The Guadalupe Mountains of Texas

NUMBER TEN
The Elma Dill Russell Spencer Foundation Series

Michael Allender
© '80

The Guadalupe Mountains of Texas

PHOTOGRAPHS
AND DRAWINGS BY
MICHAEL ALLENDER

TEXT BY
ALAN TENNANT

UNIVERSITY OF TEXAS PRESS   Austin

Copyright © 1980 by the University of Texas Press
All rights reserved
Printed in the United States of America
by The Whitley Company, Austin, Texas.

Requests for permission to reproduce material
from this work should be sent to
    Permissions,
    University of Texas Press,
    Box 7819, Austin, Texas 78712.

Library of Congress Cataloging in Publication Data

Tennant, Alan, 1943–
    The Guadalupe Mountains of Texas.

    1. Guadalupe Mountains National Park. 2. Natural history—
Texas—Guadalupe Mountains National Park.
I. Allender, Michael, 1947–   II. Title
F392.G86T46   917.64'94   80-16821
ISBN 0-292-72720-8

Second Printing, 1981

FRONTISPIECE:
Roadrunner (*Geococcyx californianus*)
and collared lizard (*Crotaphytus collaris*)

To Jeannie and Susan

Maple leaves in McKittrick Creek.
Nikon FE. 28 mm Nikor lens.
Kodachrome.

Acknowledgments

Our thanks to

Harry Lord
Chris Lynch
Mike Mayer
Roger Reisch
Joe Vinson
Caroline Wilson

The Photographer's Preface

To step into the folds of the Guadalupe Mountains, or into any wild place as a photographer, and go through the motions of making a telling, poignant statement on film is to have an experience utterly saturated with endless stimuli. Every facet of one's surroundings impinges its own brand of *image* on the human sensory systems. The wind, screaming up from the canyon floor, laden with tiny ice crystals, stings the face. It is laced with the pungent fragrance of pine needles, of the sap rising in the sun-warmed limbs. Underfoot the rotting snow gives way to the rush of spring. A myriad of migrating warblers throw their excited voices into the fray. The light of the early morning sun spreads across the canvas, enveloping all that it touches in a warm glow, while the shadows—to the trained eye—reflect the azure of an empty sky.

The observer is entertained by the *entire* symphony. It is the sum of the parts that creates the mood, stimulates the mind and eye, makes the whole. But the camera and film are not so sensitive as the mind. When all is said and done, and the photographic process is completed, the viewer is presented with a two-dimensional abstraction of shapes, lines, light values, and spaces. However much information is there, it cannot hope to convey the many stimuli, the mood, the feeling that moved the photographer to press the shutter. This is where all the training and experience the photographer has at his command must be put to use, to isolate the parts from the whole, to separate the visual from the auditory, tactual, and olfactory, and find a way to present the visual in a self-supporting role. The physical act of taking a photograph (especially if the image is the reversed, upside down one of a view camera) forces one to look. In making the images for this volume, I tried to go beyond that, by isolating, feeling, thinking, and, I hope, in the end, seeing.

Michael Allender

South McKittrick Canyon from McKittrick Ridge.
Arca Swiss 4 × 5. 210 mm Schneider lens.
Ektachrome.

Ponderosa pine cones and maple
leaves dress the autumn floor of Pine
Spring Canyon.
Arca Swiss 4 × 5. 90 mm Schneider lens.
Ektachrome.

Cloud-covered desert from Pine Top
campsite.
Arca Swiss 4 × 5. 210 mm Schneider lens.
Ektachrome.

1

December 1, 1978

Harry and Sharla Lord walked into McKittrick Canyon at dusk in a light shower of snowflakes. By the time they reached their home, Pratt Lodge, half-way up the canyon, there was an inch of unmarked new snow in the yard. A little later, Harry went out to check his thermometer and saw a line of big wet pawprints just beyond the porch. A cougar had padded by, headed down the trail, passing within fifteen feet of the house.

—GUADALUPE MOUNTAINS NATIONAL PARK
WILDLIFE FILE: MAMMALS

ALONG U.S. 180 some ten miles northeast of Guadalupe Mountains National Park, there is a singular sight for this country. A lone Arizona ash stands by the pavement, one of only three or four trees along the highway for forty miles in either direction. It is no more than fifteen feet high, with a seven-inch trunk, but the presence of any tree at all in this bleak terrain stirs a need for outlines softer than the hard vistas of rock and sage stretching across the plains. The tree has also stirred the merchandising imperative of the KOA company, which has erected two garish signs next to it. They promise, twenty miles hence, "Grass for [picture of tent]" and "400 Trees [two pictured]." The vegetation-hungry travelers at whom this message is aimed are within eight miles of dense stands of Douglas fir, aspen, ponderosa pine, and big tooth maple, but the forest is high above them, unsuspected, beyond the lip of the Guadalupe escarpment. From the highway, a thin frieze of trees is visible along the rimrock, but from these few wind-warped stragglers, it is impossible to imagine that the valleys beyond hide a Rocky Mountain forest, living in the cool moisture of the Pacific clouds rolling past, a mile above the spare Chihuahuan brush.

When Continental Airlines pilots knock back the throttles on their 727's for the hundred-mile glide into El Paso International, they are just under fourteen thousand feet, some five miles east of the Guadalupe Mountains. The rumpled brown rug two miles below is a northern loop of the Chihuahuan Desert. As I watch this strip of barren earth slide past my porthole, suddenly there are trees up close, seemingly just under the wings. A dark, wooded island thrusts upward,

Raccoon (*Procyon lotor*) and Rio Grande leopard frog (*Rana berlandieri*)

occupying nearly half of what was airspace an instant before. We are passing over the Guadalupe escarpment, jutting far up out of the desert floor. For less than a minute, the forest and meadow of the high plateau are close below. Then the sharp edge of the western scarp slices across the conifers with two thousand feet of sheer precipice, and the earth again drops away from our aluminum floor. It is a wonderful moment, reminding me of Amazon bush pilots winging over a remote crater of remnant dinosaurs hidden in the depths of the Mato Grosso.

Dramatic as the Guadalupes' topography is from the air, however, from the desert itself—where one would imagine the cliffs to be over-whelming—there is little visual impact. In most places, the palisades are so far away from the highway that they look no larger than the myriad smaller bluffs, a hundred feet high, that fill the foreground between scarp and road. For the most part, the Guadalupe cliffs' dramatic plunge from montane conifer forest to bleached salt flat goes unperceived. Only El Capitan stands out, looking a tenth its true size.

Thousands of cars climb through the pass that notches the moun-tains' spine just below this mile-high headland, but few passengers realize that they are threading their way across the disjunct, south-ernmost tip of the Rocky Mountains. Like the bowsprit of a broad-beamed ship, El Capitan's stark monolith joins the southern ends of the two long Guadalupe escarpments, whose sheer rock faces have sealed off the high country from the surrounding desert since the mountains' birth. On top, the montane plateau is flat only in relation to its sheer sides, for the high country is so wrinkled with dozens of crenellated canyons that, from the air, the peaks look like a wedge of giant green molars. Both east and west scarps angle northward into New Mexico, the western side stretching fifty-six miles to Cleaver County, while the somewhat shorter eastern scarp peters out in the rolling hills below Carlsbad Caverns.

Originally, the Guadalupe Mountains were the hills surrounding the upper Guadalupe River near Kerrville, but an eighteenth-century map copier's error shifted the name four hundred miles northwest to the front range of the Rockies, whose lower end fingers southward from Colorado and New Mexico. Most of the Guadalupe Mountains are in New Mexico, in fact, and Guadalupe Mountains National Park includes only the highest and driest tip of the range, where it crosses the state line into Texas. The New Mexico portion of the Guadalupes, including some of the mountains' best deciduous woodland, is Lincoln National Forest.

Although its vertical palisades suggest violent seismic upheaval, only in the most gradual geological sense was the Guadalupe cordillera ever actually lifted. The peaks look and feel like the Rockies, sharing much of their flora and fauna, but the two ranges are not structurally related, since the Rockies are the buckled-up edges of colliding conti-nental plates, while the Guadalupes are the product of erosion nibbling away at elevated tableland. During the Permian period, most of West Texas was sea floor, while northern South America filled the Caribbean, with Venezuela and Honduras-Guatemala beached along the Gulf Coast. Then, starting 165 million years ago, a slow balancing of the continental masses, sliding inexorably across the lithic putty beneath, made an adjustment to the buildup of dense sediments then flowing into both the Gulf of Mexico and the nearby Rio Grande rift by squeezing the lighter rock of the old West Texas seabed upward to form a high inland plateau. Conifer forests covered the uplands at first, during both late Permian and early Triassic time, but real mountains were created out of the new plateau only when the mud and sand that encased the reef during the latter part of its ocean-floor tenure weathered away. The Guadalupes did not join the surrounding sedimentary matrix in sliding off, down drainage channels into the alluvial soils of Central Texas and northern Mexico, because the peaks are harder.

They are harder because they were made by living creatures. The first were lime-secreting algae, filtering down an eons-long rain of fine calcareous dust. Then, building on the precipitated remains of the algae, tiny shelled brachiopods and coral polyps, steadily cementing together their intricate shell homes, eventually built a narrow reef thirty miles long, whose builders died when the reef was smothered with the detritus of erosion from the ancestral Rocky Mountains. Left untended by the lime-secreting polyps, the lacy avenues of their empty coral apartments gradually dissolved into a diagenetic solution of lime and magnesium carbonates that remained sealed within the surrounding sedimentary fill. Eventually, the solution recrystallized into a hard limestone bar, thousands of feet thick, the remnant of which now looms a mile above the eroded Trans-Pecos plain.

A little of this sedimentary covering remains as a coarse shell sand of mollusk fragments, still visible in thin sections of the limestone, while imprints of the animals themselves—crinoids, fusulinids, clams, and brachiopods—pock a stony matrix known as micrite. Deeper in the reef, where diagenetic solution has not melted away the limestone's original capillary structure, traces of its ancient coral filigree remain. Almost all of the gray crusty limestone which makes up the Guadalupe peaks once had this structure, but the lower layers formed by earlier coral colonies have been so thoroughly dissolved and redeposited by the interstitial drainage of rainwater that the stenciled lines of the polyps' walled homes were obliterated long ago. Pieces of more recent reefs, however, especially those of the caprock, are cut and polished to show the network of interlacing coral pores—each cell now filled with hardened dust—that lie hidden beneath the rocks' ordinary chalky exteriors. In other dry enclaves that escaped the fluid-homogenization process, chunks of the dark limestone are traced with lighter outlines left by the skeletons of calcareous sponges, whose remains also make up much of the periphery of Capitan reef.

A mile beyond its palisades, I stand on the old abyssal plain. Sharks were the only animals that lived in the depths here, for the first leviathans—reptilian marine plesiosaurs—were still seventy million years away in the future, the first whales nearly a hundred million years after that, when these scarps first breathed as a living coral wall. It is not easy to visualize, even after seeing the beautiful model of this community of tubular corals, sponges, and serpentine worms that is sandwiched between exhibits of Model-T era oilfield technology and petrochemical public relations displays at the Petroleum Museum in Midland. Later, from the end of the Leonardian to the Chidruan Epoch, taller reefs flowered here and covered the arid bluffs with the fleshy strainer flanges of the polyps that lived in the sunlit shallows, looking much the same as their descendants in today's tropic seas, for the coral community is the earth's oldest complex ecosystem. Although the rock faces seem lifeless now, dry and crumbly, in places miniature wildflowers—purplish rock-crevice milkworts (*Polygala rimulicola*) and mat dwarf daisies (*Chaetoppa hersheyi*) with white-petalled blossoms less than a quarter-inch across—push right out of the limestone.

Ninety million years after Capitan reef flourished here, shallow lagoons and marshes again covered West Texas, and in them lived dinosaurs. Some were pterosaurs, or pterodactyls, and one species, *Titanopteryx*, was the largest animal that ever flew. Although almost certainly warm blooded, and possibly covered with fur, it was a reptile, and it was as large as a jet fighter. Its remains were discovered in the Javelina deposits of Big Bend National Park in 1971 and immediately set off worldwide headlines, both because of the size of the creature—vindicating a dozen Japanese monster movies—and because everyone's fancy was caught by the intriguing theory of its finder, University of Texas graduate student Douglas Lawson (who, with characteristic paleontological flair, named the animal *Quetzalcoatlus* after the Aztec plumed serpent god, only to have it revised to *Titanopteryx* some eight years later), that his big flying reptile was a sort of saurian vulture, using its nine-foot neck to probe the innards of dinosaur carcasses. Dr. Wann Langston, leader of the expedition, told me how that theory came about.

"We had found a very large brontosaurus skeleton, which was holding up a small hill. In the course of excavating it, I had crawled inside the rib cage to scoop away more dirt and was still in there looking out through the ribs when Lawson came trotting up. This pterosaur discovery was fresh in his mind, and it just popped into his head that that long neck would be just the thing to reach in and take a bite of me."

Dr. Langston is strongly inclined toward debunking fanciful theories, and he thinks that the giant-scavenger hypothesis is one of them. From a row of cabinets at the University of Texas Balcones Research Center, he withdrew a pair of pterosaur mandibles, three feet long and very slender, with flattened, spoonlike tips. "See if you could eat a dinosaur with those," he challenged. There were plenty of fossilized carcasses at hand, but I decided not to try to dismember any of them with the spindly chopsticks. Langston believes the 65-million-year-old reptile was an aquatic, possibly marine, predator which fed on small, live prey. It may have probed the banks of those shallow West Texas marshes for the big burrowing worms and arthropods that lived there,

Upper South McKittrick Canyon.
Arca Swiss 4 × 5. 90 mm Schneider lens. Ektachrome.

but its long neck would have seen better service, and brought in larger prey for the creature's high-powered metabolism, if *Titanopteryx* had glided along just above the waves, periodically stabbing downward, like a black skimmer with an anhinga's extendable neck, to snatch mackerel-sized fish from beneath the surface. The aerial dexterity required for this would have been considerable, though, and the way in which *Titanopteryx* may have managed it is part of an ongoing controversy over how pterosaurs were able to fly at all.

The first three-foot shoulder bone that Lawson scraped out of the side of a crumbly Big Bend arroyo was so massive that he had no idea it could have belonged to a flying creature until analysis at the Vertebrate Paleontology Laboratory in Austin revealed that the huge bone had once been hollow, with paper-shell walls less than an eighth of an inch thick. "Only four kinds of animals have extremely hollow bones," Langston wrote, "'ostrich' dinosaurs, birds, . . . pterosaurs, and some fish. Fish this bone was not, nor could it have belonged to an 'ostrich' dinosaur whose bones had somewhat thicker walls."* Birds use a different flight mechanism—hence different joint articulation—so Lawson's humerus had to belong to a pterosaur, although it was probably connected to the animal's respiratory system, as are the tubular flight bones of birds.

The world comes at you a lot faster when you fly, and processing so much new visual data quickly enough to make flight corrections in time required a brain more complex than any that had evolved so far, relatively larger than other dinosaurs, and nearly proportionate in size to modern birds. (Despite their big brains and similar hollow-bone respiratory structure, pterosaurs were not ancestral to birds. Birds evolved instead from a much earlier group of chicken-sized Jurassic dinosaurs that ran around on long, slender hind legs like small ostriches. Their forelimbs had extended fingers with flattened scales that they used like fans to scoop insects toward their hooked beaks. Today, hawks use a similar maneuver. They mantle, or cup, their fanned-out wings and tail into a stiff little tent that they droop over their prey. If the mouse wriggles free of the talons, it is fenced in by a picket of feathers in every direction except forward, under the hooked beak. Eventually, those flat finger scales thinned and faceted into primary feathers, which the little dinosaurs could flail rapidly enough to take off on short, Wright Brothers hops. Like tailless kites, they had no directional stability, though, until the scales along the sides of their tails also spread out into the thin, flexible flanges that eventually became feathers. At this point, the creature was *Archaeopteryx*, the first bird.)

Forty million years later, *Titanopteryx* also had trouble getting off the ground. It is generally accepted that, as advanced, warm-blooded reptiles, the smaller pterosaurs had high enough metabolisms to fly away from their perches like bats, but *Titanopteryx*'s size and chunky build may have limited it to gravity-assisted take-off plunges from tall

Upper South McKittrick Canyon.
Arca Swiss 4 × 5. 90 mm Schneider lens.
Ektachrome.

*Wann Langston, Jr., "The Great Pterosaur," *Discovery*, March 1978, p. 21. [Office of the Vice-President for Research, University of Texas at Austin]

bluffs. There were no tall bluffs anywhere near the lowland estuarine setting of the Javelina Formation, however, although the tall redwood trees that grew there may have afforded high enough perches for a glide out over the water. But what if *Titanopteryx* forgot about its subsequent take-off and happened to land on flat ground? To get its three-hundred-pound bulk into the air required more energy than the big reptile's metabolism should have been capable of expending, and to keep it there took fifty-foot wings that aviation engineers doubt could have withstood the flight stresses. Little of the creature's structural anatomy fits the models of either paleontologists or aircraft designers. But, then, bumblebees are theoretically unable to fly, too.

Somehow, it must have been managed. The puzzle intrigues Wann Langston and has inspired him to become an amateur aviation theorist. Tracks preserved in Arizona sandstones indicate that pterosaurs were able to scramble along on all fours like grounded bats, and on flat terrain *Titanopteryx* probably used that technique, giving everything it had to attain a lumbering lift-off speed. Langston imagines this as a Brob-dingnagian version of the paddling charge of the albatross, which also must run desperately into the wind to get aloft. Once airborne, by flexing its enormously elongated fingers, *Titanopteryx* could vary the tension of its wing membranes enough to increase lift or lose it, like hauling or luffing a sail into the wind. Before flight stresses built too high, it could simply spill some wind from its wings and give up a little altitude. Using this variable-membrane-tension approach to skim low over the water, the big reptile could surf on the billows of wind thrown up by surface rollers, stretching and loosening the leathery sheets between its long fingers to take just the right purchase on every upward surge and maintain an ideal fishing altitude three or four feet above the water.

The succession of seas that battered the ocean side of Capitan reef, and later fringed its estuarine marshes, have been gone as long as the dinosaurs, drained away to the east into the Atlantic basin. In their place, after the assault of eighty million winters of ice and rain against its earthen shroud, the reef has appeared again, reaching up to tap the cloud-borne moisture hanging above the desert. It is the Guadalupes' second time around as an oasis, but its evergreen forest—which harbors Texas' only chipmunks (gray-footed), elk, cougars, and even black bears—is slowly dying. It has done this many times since the Miocene, however, as successive ice sheets advanced and retreated, drawing their moisture away to the north and shrinking the suddenly dessicated co-nifer woodlands into disjunct island stands atop the highest plateaus, separated by expanses of new desert grassland.

Because the current dry spell is of recent origin, at least in biolog-ical terms, the prevailing plants and animals here are still primarily moist-environment forms that flourished when the Trans-Pecos was a wetter, cooler place and that lately have been forced to alter their ecological strategies as the land dried out around them.

Eroded limestone spires in South McKittrick Canyon.
Arca Swiss 4 × 5. 210 mm Schneider lens. Ektachrome.

Among the plants, the most successful adaptors to desert life have been the cacti, although most Chihuahuan vegetation has developed similarly thorny characteristics. "Everything that grows west of the Pecos either sticks, stings, or stinks," the cowhands' saying went; and many do worse than that. Despite Gene Autrey's theme, the lowly jimson weed seldom scrved as feed for the Longhorns, because it is a highly toxic member of the nightshade family. *Datura wrightii*, the species found in the Guadalupes, has tubular white flowers that bloom from late spring through the fall, when it produces large, deadly green fruits covered with spikes and called thornapples. All parts of the jimson weed are poisonous, but today its victims are usually backpackers trying to hallucinate on the seeds.

In contrast, and in spite of the hostile, spiny prospect they offer, cacti have directed more evolutionary effort toward dealing with the desert climate than toward resisting foragers: the thorns that cover every inch of most kinds are there only partly to protect the plant from being eaten. Before cacti adapted to desert life, their spines were leaves, lavishly transpiring water into a more humid atmosphere. Since all plants lose most of their water in this way, shaping their leaves into hardened spikes served both to ward off grazing animals and, more importantly, to cut evaporation to a minimum. But closing off their transpiration surfaces also meant giving up the leaves' wide, photosynthetic layers, and the cacti were forced to make their food in the skin of their green stems—which evolved a waxy, watertight armor and enlarged to hold the maximum amount of water (often in expandable accordion folds like those of the Sonoran saguaro, organ, and barrel cacti), as well as to offer more chlorophyll-enriched stalk surface to the sun. Only New World plants made these adaptations, and (except for a single distant cousin, *Rhipsalis*, found in Madagascar and Ceylon) cacti do not live in the older deserts of Asia, Africa, and Australia.

Far above the plains, now, the conifer forest—a remnant of the dense Pleistocene woodland that once stretched northward to the Arctic treeline—hangs on still, cool and green for the most part but also dry. West Texas is still drying out, and even above seven thousand feet, the clouds carry less moisture every year—too little for the woodland to replenish itself. Already, the aspens are confined to well-shaded valleys deep in the mountains and an arid juniper scrub may soon fill the highland bowl where Douglas fir now stand.

While the old forest flourished here, sometimes spreading out across the savannah below the escarpment, the age of mammals reached its peak. Broad evergreen forests grew everywhere across the great plains in the chill, moist path of the advancing glaciers, spreading hundreds of miles ahead of the ice. The ice never reached Texas, but the conifer woodland it pushed southward brought Arctic animals, including musk oxen, to the Guadalupe high country, where their remains are still occasionally found in Williams Cave, probably carried there by saber-toothed cats (*smilodon*), along with the remains of the cats themselves, zebras, ground sloths, and the scavenging hyenas and dire wolves (*Canis dirus*) that ultimately fed on all of them. Although it is surrounded by desert now, just below the western face of El Capitan, during the Pleistocene, the cave opened onto a mesic forest-and-savannah countryside that supported some wonderfully exotic herbivores: the North American rhinocerous, mammoths, and strange chalicotheres with their great defensive hooked claws instead of hooves. Herds of long-horned *Bison attenuatus* and *B. occidentalis*, ancestors of the animals that fed the plains Indians, grazed across a veldlike Trans-Pecos, preyed upon by dire wolves and *Arctodus*, the two-thousand-pound Pleistocene grizzly. Horses also first reached their present form on these western plains before migrating to Europe across an early land bridge linking a warmer Greenland to Scotland, not to be seen again in North America for fifty million years. (They returned with the Spaniards during the sixteenth and seventeenth centuries, but camels—llamas, really, that also evolved here later than the horses and then departed from the opposite corner of North America, over the dry Bering straits to Asia—didn't make their re-entry until two hundred years later, when the U.S. Army Camel Corps was set up at Camp Verde in Kerr County during the 1850's. The camels were farmed out to West Texas as desert freighters and performed well in the Trans-Pecos, ferrying supplies along the big bend of the Rio Grande between the army posts at Castolon and Presidio, where they exhibited only slightly worse temperaments than the most obnoxious mules. In spite of their great endurance and ability to get by on marginal fodder, however, within a few years the railroads rendered their overland, heavy-cargo-hauling capabilities obsolete, and several bunches were released or escaped into the desert, where they were the cause of sensational sightings for years. The Arabian handlers imported with the camels fared somewhat better: they learned Spanish and blended homogeneously into the border community.)

With the nearly simultaneous coming of man and the desert, the herds withered away, and with them went the predators and scavengers. The white-winged eagle-vultures that lived here for thirty million years are extinct, and the last condors are dying in southern California, hemmed in by freeways and housing developments, although once both were plentiful on these cliffs and from their rimrock eyries rode the morning thermals out over the prairie herds, spiraling down to blanket the previous night's kills in croaking flocks. In 1910, at the end of his first day on the African veld, Teddy Roosevelt is supposed to have bellowed, "A Pleistocene day! By God, it's still here." Now, even golden eagles—recent victims of shotgunning from light planes—are rare along the Guadalupe scarps.

A view from a ridge above South
McKittrick Canyon, looking along
the eastern escarpment.
Arca Swiss 4 × 5. 90 mm Schneider lens.
Ektachrome.

Alligator juniper in Pine Spring
Canyon.
Arca Swiss 4 × 5. 90 mm Schneider lens.
Ektachrome.

2

May 20, 1978

Observation for 15 minutes—1:15 P.M.—lion first seen on top of Shady Bluff Ridge. Lion worked its way from end of ridge to junction with main east-west ridge of Pine Canyon . . . topped the ridge approximately 250 yards from Pine Canyon trailhead. Appeared to be full-grown adult. He followed a deer trail up to the ridge. From the way he moved, I felt he had been there before. Topped the ridge and headed into South McKittrick drainage.

—M. MAYER, RANGER
GUADALUPE MOUNTAINS NATIONAL PARK
WILDLIFE FILE: MAMMALS

IN PARK HEADQUARTERS, the wildlife file has a section for each species recorded here. Even the rarer animals have eight or ten index entries. The peregrine falcons are unusual but famous, and there is a two-inch stack of index cards filed behind their heading. There are no entries for golden eagles. The single resident recorded here now sits, stuffed, in a glass box in the visitor center. The label reads: "This young golden eagle was found dying of starvation near one of the springs in the park. Attempts to bring him back failed. For many people, spotting a golden eagle in the open or hearing his piercing scream is the thrill of a lifetime. Federal law prohibits the killing or molesting of golden eagles."

The effectiveness of light planes against coyotes became evident during the 1930's, first in California. Terrified by the engine roar, coyotes abandon the protective crouch that would leave them invisible to a pilot skimming the sage at eighty miles an hour and make a dash for it across open terrain. They can dodge and twist, but, with no place for the coyote to hide, the men in the plane nearly always win. By 1930, J. O. Casparis had brought the idea to Alpine, Texas. A similar dirt-strip operation was started in Fort Stockton at about the same time, quickly followed by two more aerial hunting clubs at Kent and Marathon.

With so many gunners in the air, it was soon evident that golden eagles were even more vulnerable to the planes than coyotes. Floating slowly across the empty West Texas skies for hours at a time, the big birds were large enough to be spotted easily and tame enough to be approached by even those early Piper Cubs. Invincible on the wing since

Elk (*Cervus canadensis*) and mountain lion (*Felis concolor*)

their evolution in the Oligocene, eagles had never developed defenses against airborne predators and, instead of descending to the shelter of trees and canyons, most of them ignored the planes completely until a load of #2's ripped them out of the air. Occasionally, a breeding pair would try to outfly the aircraft like rival birds of prey, using the burning dives that are part of their territorial defense against other raptors. A few even scored kamikaze hits on the Super Cubs; and one Brewster County pilot was nearly downed in the late forties by an eagle that ripped out his windshield and much of the Piper's canvas fuselage in its final dive. Unfortunately, all the planes remained airworthy, however, and Casparis alone claims more than eight thousand eagle kills between 1945 and 1952.

Even in those early days, the schizoid nature of the hunts was evident. Ostensibly, the motivation was economic: protect the lambs and kid goats from predation. But flying time went for twenty-eight dollars an hour and, in the thirties, six hours in the air cost more than the lambs an eagle could eat all winter. Never a utilitarian extermination service, from the very beginning the main objective was obvious. All the aerial hunting was done by clubs—sporting associations patterned after the original Brewster County Eagle and Coyote Club, whose atmosphere was one of glamor and risky sport. (The risk was much larger in barnstorming the hills for coyotes, and quite a few crack-ups occurred, mainly in Colorado and Utah. It sounded better to call them wolves, though—a canid puffery which is still the norm everywhere in the West. In a region where wolves have not lived for sixty years, the South Texas Wolf Hunters Association is pained to acknowledge that its members—with their hundreds of specialized hounds—kill coyotes. It's just not the same. Throughout the state, ranchers call small coyotes coyotes, and big ones wolves. But there are no wild lobos left anywhere in Texas, and only a few dozen red wolves, genetically diluted with coyote inbreeding. All of them live in a small area of coastal rice fields between Houston and Beaumont.)

Golden eagles know no such boundaries. Because of their size, they seldom occupy an established home range, since almost no contiguous territory is rich enough in prey to support a pair throughout the year. Except for nesting, eagles are gypsies, wandering hundreds of miles in great geographical arcs as the seasons turn. Rather than migrants, they are nomads. The young bald eagles fledged during February in Florida may spend June fishing along the St. Lawrence, while from the old eyries on the Guadalupe cliffs, young golden eagles soared northward as far as the Snake River gorge. In winter, the birds flowed down the north-south valleys of the Rockies to the southern extremity of their mountain habitat in northern Mexico. Since they are able to cover up to two hundred miles in a day with favorable winds, and can fast for two or three weeks, local food supplies offer little constraint to eagles, and they may turn up almost anywhere above the twenty-third parallel, although the birds shot out of the airfields in Kent, Alpine, Marathon, and Fort Stockton were mainly locally fledged adolescents from the Guadalupe and Davis Mountains. They nearly vanished in West Texas during the late fifties, and for the last twenty-five years the hunts have been directed at northern eagles wintering in Central Texas.

Around the first of each year, eagles from Canada and the northern Rockies drift down across the Edwards Plateau on a more easterly line, crossing the Rio Grande and traveling as far as Guanajuato, Hidalgo, and Nuevo León before swinging north again, a month later. In February, for reasons of which no one is sure, the largest concentration of both golden and bald eagles in North America occurs around Rocksprings and Uvalde, where, in spite of federal protection, the birds are shot from helicopters. The notorious Eagle Ranch indictments in 1978 resulted in the government's first successful prosecution on behalf of the eagles, but the professional extermination firm which flew the helicopters was issued another aerial hunting permit by the Texas Department of Parks and Wildlife four months after the trial. Like the original permit, it was limited to coyotes—the only way a professional hunter can legally fly around with a shotgun poked through his helicopter's doorway.

Helicopters do an even better job on eagles than the elaborate, big-prop Waco and Steerman biplanes developed for aerial hunting during the last days of the sporting eagle shoots, because they are more maneuverable. Unlike the modified crop dusters, helicopters can hover low enough to hit even roosting birds and then set down to check their kills. But, with their specialized pilots and two hundred dollars an hour flight time, helicopters are too expensive—and, with the newly enforced federal laws, too risky—for even ranch-baron sportsmen, so that almost all the eagles shot from the choppers have been downed by professional hunters ostensibly gunning for coyotes. The expense is absurd, but the old predator folklore is fueled by a couple of new, market-determined factors. Most of the Chicano shepherds—who used to search out the best grazing for their owners' flocks—now have diplomas and good jobs in town. With the flocks more or less on their own, the herdsmen's traditional search for good pastures is out of the question, and each year's batch of lambs must now be started early enough for them to reach market size by July, when the long barbs of speargrass harden in the winter and spring pastures where they were born, stabbing the sheep's noses and forcing the ranchers to sell all but the breeding stock they can afford to feed, penned, until fall. The early start means that the lambs must be born in mid-winter, however, just when the big concentration of eagles arrives in the hill country.

But February is a bad time to be a newborn lamb on the open range, even without eagles, and northers kill a large percentage of each year's crop. Many of the lambs are scavenged by eagles, which, when jackrabbits are scarce, sit around in blatant groups, feeding on the carcasses like beautiful vultures, showing far too much gall for their own good. Seemingly unable to develop much fear of man, when eagles move into an area they are anything but secretive, sailing boldly back and forth over the low canyons and pastures and perching enormously in the tallest trees. Not surprisingly, all dead lambs—and there are a lot of them after every cold snap—are presumed to be eagle kills. No study of raptor predation on sheep has yet been done in Texas, in spite of the furor, primarily because the eagles are so transient here, with such a constant turnover in residency, that few individuals remain for the entire six weeks the birds annually spend on the Edwards Plateau. It was not until early 1978 that the first photograph of an eagle actually hitting a newborn lamb—in this case, a staked-out pet named Charlene—was obtained by Scott Campbell, a reporter on special assignment for the *San Angelo Standard-Times*.

To many residents whose income depends on the wool and mohair yield, this picture confirmed the eagles as villains; and villains are what the sheep and goat business needs right now. The once highly profitable enterprise is sinking rapidly in the face of competition from synthetic fibers—Texas' largest mohair processing plant, in Abilene, closed in March of 1979—and birds of prey have become the focus of the frustrations of angry stockmen caught between their desire for federal subsidies and their resentment of the government protection of the eagles that accompanies the payments. Even at their worst, eagles don't kill very many sheep, but it is important for some of the ranchers to believe they could control their economic problems with a twelve-gauge solution.

By February 1980, however, the stockmen had developed a cheaper and more sophisticated method for getting rid of their eagles and even won some favorable publicity. Fifty-six of the wintering birds were caught alive in padded snap-jaw raccoon traps for release in South Texas, where they were supposed to move on down the coast into Mexico. (Although there are more people and farms, and consequently less natural habitat below the Rio Grande than above it, the myth still persists that Mexico is mecca for wildlife, and dumping release animals near the border is generally accepted as a good thing. This was also planned for the sheep-killing Guadalupe cougars, had any of them ever fallen to a tranquilizer dart.) Although some of the trapped eagles survived the leg damage inflicted by the trap jaws and the week-long wait in crates before shipment to the Aransas Refuge, none were seen again after release, when they were too weak to have much chance in hunting the few jackrabbits living on the edge of the coastal marshes. The additional aerial handicap of big gaps cut from their wing and tail pinions in order to identify any that might return to the hill country made sure that none of the eagles—mostly clumsily flying, first-year adolescents—ever did so.

During the height of the aerial range war, a female golden eagle was shot down near the Rio Grande a hundred miles south of the park. Both wings were crimped, but she survived and was living a gladiator's life when I found her, battling cats thrown into her four-foot-square cage for food. Sometimes there were several at once. She was undefeated but not unscathed, especially psychologically, for when I released her into a fifty-foot-square enclosure she battered back and forth against the walls in a ceaseless frenzy and I knew I had to use the avian equivalent of a straitjacket: the falconer's leather hood and jesses. Hooded and unable to see, a panicked raptor immediately calms down and, tethered with a long leash attached to padded anklets, or jesses, cannot reach anything to slam against. Like all birds of prey, the female is larger than the male, and beneath feathered ankles half the size of my wrists her thick yellow toes stretched nine inches between long black talons. Catching the leather (Tandy's toughest cowhide) between them, she ripped the first set of jesses apart as easily as she would slice open a jackrabbit. Infuriated, she lunged and screamed through the puny minnow seine I had used to net her. A Russian falconer was actually killed by a golden eagle not long ago, when the bird sank its talons into his throat, and this one seemed to have the same idea. As I lay in the mud, grasping the now tetherless shanks while the eagle flailed above me, the parable of the man who rode the tiger took on a vividness that hadn't occurred to me before.

The melee was watched by my partner: photographer, artist, and semi—mountain man Michael Allender, who at this point reluctantly took off his belt and began to whittle. As the second set of jesses slowly took shape, I could hear him talking softly in the intervals between the eagle's screams.

"I'm hurrying. I know you're miserable, but I'm going as fast as I can." Glumly, I realized he was talking to the bird. He watched the big hooked beak rip out a piece of my collar. "May not ever be happy again," Michael sighed.

"You can't say an animal is happy to a biologist," he told me later. "I had to write in my thesis that my coyote pups 'swung their tails laterally' when I played with them." There were five little coyotes, research subjects for his wildlife biology thesis, although Allender was more interested in them as cohorts. Whipsnade, Alpine, Fuzzy, Rema, and Baby were dug out of a den which Michael located by sticking his head down lots of burrows and listening for whimpers. Whipsnade was his favorite and was named after the London zoo with its famous collection of wild canids. Baby was weak and soon eaten by the other pups.

Baby's gruesome end at the fangs of his brothers and sisters was important to me, because I had lost young coyotes in the same way. At one time, I was saddled with a group of orphans confiscated by game wardens from roadside peddlers in North Texas. There were two gunshot redtail hawks, a swashbuckling one-winged great horned owl, a young skunk, a raccoon with abcessed palms, and a litter of thirteen coyote pups, each individually boxed in a cardboard carton, all assembled in the rear seat of a blue Dodge Polara rented from Avis. The coyote cartons only lasted a few minutes. The raccoon and skunk were secure in protective metal cages, and the raptors were too fierce to mess with, but the next day in Austin, in spite of two Gainesburgers each, the coyote litter had shrunk to eleven pups with bloated bellies.

Michael wasn't surprised. For awhile, during babyhood, any coyote which can't hold its own apparently ceases to be perceived as a litter mate by its siblings and is seen instead as something alien but alive, and small: therefore, prey. This never happens with adult coyotes, however. Like wolves, coyote clans depend on a rigid social caste to regulate both their family life and the cooperative hunting tactics they need to survive. Jackrabbits are faster and more maneuverable than any coyote and are consequently almost impossible for a lone hunter to catch on his own, so that family teamwork is the only sure way to get a meal; and every member is needed for success. Consequently, the alpha wolf will kill an intruding coyote but not one of his own clan, no matter how weak. Until Allender took up with his coyotes, no one knew what mechanism shut off the aggressor and why it only worked with grown animals.

As a zoology graduate student at Texas A&M, Michael heard about an unusual program at the University of Utah, whose first researcher had vanished not long before, along with all his coyotes. Jack London dancing in his head, Michael agreed to fill the vacant slot. He found Dr. Dietland Muellerschwartz, whose heated pursuit of the urine-borne glandular scent missives known as pheromones, Allender learned, had driven his assistant over the brink. The man shot some of Muellerschwartz's coyotes and high-tailed it into the countryside with the rest of the pack. Another research assistant came and left quickly, in dismay. Allender was to take up where they had left off.

Because coyote pheromones never held any interest for him, Michael never tried to collect any of the assigned specimens, although he remembers that the prescribed procedure involved a lot of urine and was unpleasant for both coyote and researcher. It was a strategy that had apparently never occurred to his predecessors. Instead, as Muellerschwartz fumed and ranted, threatening to cut off his nonexistent funding, Allender bottle-raised the four remaining pups and watched them develop a social hierarchy. At first, although none was weak enough to invite Baby's fate, until they reached three months of age all that the pups could manage in their personal relationships was a sort of stalemate. Then a new pattern developed in their fighting. The defeated animal, lying vulnerable on its back, would press its hind feet up against the lower belly and flanks of the winner standing over it, somehow forestalling the impending flurry of snaps and causing the top dog to gradually relax and take on a slightly glazed expression. Visiting coyotes from another student's litter showed Michael that only family members pressed each other's stomachs in this way, instinctively pawing upward at their dominant siblings, searching for the tranquilizing center that terminated aggression. The lesser animal lived but challenged less often after its close shave, and the caste relationship solidified. Based largely on consistently winning their food bowl scuffles, Fuzzy and Alpine became dominant in the Allender pack, while Whipsnade and Rema, who were better at the loser's inguinal pawing, took subordinate roles. At least for awhile.

After the pups' pecking order stabilized, Michael wanted to test the continuity of their caste positions, and, to shake things up, he re-

North McKittrick Canyon from a ridge in Lincoln National Forest. Nikon FE. 80–200 mm Nikor lens. Kodachrome.

moved Alpine, who had been giving the subordinate female a hard time anyway, promoting Rema to her vacant alpha slot. After four weeks of Rema's stardom, Michael walked into the coyote pen carrying Alpine in his arms, expecting one coyote or the other to back down after a bit of growling threat display. Instead, he sparked what would have been a battle to the death. The solidarity of the family hierarchy and the placating inguinal pawing were abandoned as the coyotes lunged for each other. Whipsnade and Fuzzy stood by, watching, as Allender was swept into the maelstrom of clicking jaws that he had inadvertently set off— charting with certainty the far limit of the inguinal cease-fire. Alpine was being thoroughly mauled by her sister, but Michael ripped her loose and cleared the gate still holding her in his equally shredded arms, leaving Rema snarling at the amazed males.

Coyotes are common in Guadalupe Mountains National Park, and three or four of them, making as much racket as a kennelful of coonhounds, tune up behind the Frijole Ranger Station on cool nights, moonlit nights, foggy nights, or whenever the mood strikes them. The complexity of their cries has a ventriloquial quality. If they are really excited, it is almost impossible to tell how many coyotes you are listening to, or where they are. This helps to confuse the sound-sensitive jackrabbits and cottontails which the hunting pack, loping abreast, one animal every twenty yards, springs from hiding. The rabbits burst away in a frantic fifty-yard dash but then, surrounded by a crescendo of yipping snarls, lose their resolve about which way to run and stop or try to double back—right into the furry explosion of a gang tackle by half the family.

Pouring in suddenly out of the black desert, the squealing cacophony always brings me upright, fighting the sleeping bag. It's not the end of the rabbit that gets me. It's the coyotes' intensity. I have no channel on which to process so much raw canine emotion—uninterpretable, yet close to my own feelings—especially far into the night, when the rational process is at its lowest ebb and visceral responses are strongest. The hour of the wolf is not physically threatening, but it finds me emotionally naked.

Michael is also a little unsettled, but with him it's nostalgia. He used to be the alpha wolf of his own gang and now he's just another dull human being, excluded from the coyotes' keen nightly enthusiasms. Allender still crunches up all the bones in his box of Colonel Sanders for their marrow if he's thinking about his pups, but it's no substitute for sprinting across the desert in a swirl of coyotes, white socks flashing through their joyful vortex like the bright shoes of a lithe high school halfback.

A few coyotes misjudge the speed of traffic on U.S. 180 and are hit by cars, but their overall number in the park, as elsewhere, is determined almost entirely by the prevailing size of the black-tailed jackrabbit population. If there are good forage and many rabbits, lots of coyotes breed and have large litters. If drought reduces the grass and forbs on which the rabbits live, only the top-ranked coyotes breed, and only two or three pups are born each year. This reproductive flexibility maintains coyotes at an equilibrium population everywhere, and only absolute loss of habitat eliminates them entirely. Traps and poison also kill a few coyotes, but the survivors learn to avoid them within a few weeks, and as long as jackrabbits and gophers are plentiful their numbers remain high, even in semisuburban areas like Los Angeles County, where, in the absence of jackrabbits, hundreds of coyotes live successfully amid the residential boulevards, foraging on garbage and pilfered dog and cat food. State and federal bounties result in lots of dead coyotes, to start with, followed by the large replacement litters of the survivors and a new equilibrium population of adaptively wary adults.

Eagle populations, in contrast, have almost no resiliency. Although a couple of pairs could, like the peregrines, presumably take advantage of protected breeding sites on the Guadalupe cliffs, the eagles' nomadic winter travels expose them to so many gunners, on foot as well as aloft, that their chances of returning year after year are small. The few eagles seen in the park now are juveniles wandering through on their adolescent transcontinental pilgrimages, rather than residents. The one I saw came floating up on the westerlies pouring through Guadalupe Pass just before dark. It looked so black against the sky that I misjudged its size and, in the distance, thought it was a raven until the bulging profile gave it away. White patches on the tail and beneath the wings showed it to be a youngster on its first fall journey across the southwest. Falconers call these adolescent wanderers passage birds, with an awareness both of their aimless travels and of their transition status between fledglings and paired adults. Unlike other raptors, eagles—especially inexperienced passage birds—frequently show no fear of man; and this one gazed coolly over at us as it sailed in off the desert, a hundred feet away, but just above our level.

Mostly, though, those invisible, mountain-thrown thermals are left to the redtailed hawks now. Eight out of ten hawks in the park are the resident redtails, which are also the most common and widespread big birds of prey everywhere in the hemisphere. First described in the West Indies over a hundred years before white men saw them in eastern North America, *Buteo jamaicensis* was expected to be a local predator in the string of islands, themselves expected to be the outlying landfall of the Orient. The species turned out to be ubiquitous from the Mexican plateau to Alaska. In winter, larger and darker races of redtails, formerly called Harlan's hawks, drift into the Guadalupe Mountains from the Rockies if heavy snow offers hiding to the rodents in their territories. They are joined, especially in the desert, by rough-legged hawks from Montana, Idaho, and the Canadian plains. Unaccustomed to man because of their remote home range, they sit tamely on roadside poles, eyeing the traffic. I recognize them by their fully feathered legs—all the way down to the toes, like eagles—and especially by the prominent yellow mandibles that extend their beaks well back into featherless, scaly-looking cheeks, giving them a distinctive, reptilian appearance. Plumed serpents.

Lying on my back, I see the bright speck for which I have been scanning the sharp-edged blue expanse above me. Through 10x optics, we are face to face. From three hundred feet, the redtail can see me just about as well as I can see her, and she dips her head to peer curiously under her wing as she floats past. She is a *buteo*, a glider. Her special province, like that of her predecessors, the pterosaurs and the condors, is buoying on the standing waves of wind thrown up by the peaks. In five minutes she is back from another direction, and this time she hangs in one spot, heading into the wind. Her aerial tactics are relevant to me because they parallel my own experience in laying wings on waves of air in gliders, light planes, and even from the earthbound end of a kite string. The flickering, swallowlike flight of the falcons is almost as alien to her life as it is to mine. Her maneuvers are slow enough to understand. She is interested and wags her head back and forth, playing with the parallax, subtly changing her depth of field as she studies me in varying focal planes. Unlike those of mammals, her eyes do not move within her skull, so she bobs and wags her head, focusing, trying different perspectives of me. My perspective is constant, and, from my perceived distance of fifty feet, she glows bright copper and cream in the sun, especially her wings which, with the light behind them, are translucent, laced with dark feather shafts and speckled with brown crosshatching.

Suspended on the rising current of air, she is anything but motionless. Her three and a half pounds are held aloft by five square feet of combined wing and tail area; but to maintain position she must move continuously. Unconsciously, she adjusts her altitude by angling the broad rectrices of her tail, automatically rotating her primaries like the fingers of extended hands—constantly searching for the perfect angle of attack on the wind in an easy little rhumba of tiny twists and corrections. I remember the crippled hawks grounded at my home in Austin: gunshot victims brought in from around the state. With beady precision they suddenly cock an eye upward, fixed on the empty sky. Seconds later, I'll hear the engine and, led by the sound, pick out the tiny silver speck that they are watching.

Once young redtails have learned to hunt, they are pretty good at it, even if they are not the totally effective killers that peregrines are, right out of the nest. The falcons are so agile that they can take any prey—often a bird in flight—at will, snacking on just a few bites from the breast. Although a redtail can't afford this luxury and eats all of its kill, few adults go hungry. This is not true of the adolescents, though, for learning to fly is a tough business, and trying to coordinate their shaky new aviation skills with the demands of nabbing a darting rodent is more than most of the young hawks can manage. During July and August there are always several of them learning to hunt around the peaks. They stoop after prey five or six times as often as the adults but score so few hits that over 80 percent starve.

35

To maintain a stable population, they have to. Nothing preys on redtails, and they can live for twenty years, during which a competent breeding pair may add fifteen new hawks to the population, where there is room for only two replacements. It is like medieval primogeniture, where the hereditary land must remain undivided to provide support for a single son, while the other siblings are forced to seek niches outside the home fief in the church, marriage, or the crusades. Young redtails strike out as passage birds, looking for an empty hunting ground, but because they are clumsy fliers at this age they are unable to look very far, or long, before they weaken from hunger, and even good hunters have only a slim chance of survival. Although adult hawks seem to be widely and randomly dispersed, raptor populations in fact operate at saturation levels determined by the capacity of the land to produce more rodents than can easily remain hidden during the day. Whether it takes one square mile or twenty to support a hawk, there is ordinarily a pair already living on every possible range, defending boundaries that intersect the next pair's territory a dozen miles away. These resident couples will sometimes tolerate the prospecting youngsters that float through their range every fall, when territorial imperatives relax and everybody does a little traveling, but by winter the nomads are squeezed out for good and will not survive unless they can find a vacancy where an old bird has fallen.

Late in August, I noticed one of these flailing adolescents, white down still trailing from his crown, make an awkward, sideways stoop onto an empty plot of ground near the park's north boundary. The young redtail was desperate for prey and ran around on the ground like a chicken, wings aloft, grabbing in vain at the swift little whiptail lizards that zipped in perfect safety between their burrows. I'm sure he didn't eat the tuna I left for him, but it was the best I could do.

Even great horned owls sometimes have trouble in the desert here. (Ordinarily, they can survive almost anywhere because their soft, flayed-edged plumage lets them fly without a rustle to drop in effortless ambush on any rodent they find in the open. A one-winged individual survived for years in Fort Worth's Forest Park, swooping down in slanting glides every night on the zoo's plentiful population of rats and then hopping from branch to branch back up into the elms.) Heading home at sunset, down the power line that runs through the western Guadalupe foothills, I noticed that one pole seemed taller than the rest. Silhouetted against the evening sky, the extension turned out to be a great horned owl, swiveling his head back and forth, watching the desert floor for signs of life. After a long, yellow-eyed look at me, he lost interest, but, perhaps because of my presence, nothing was moving near his perch. After half an hour, he still hadn't spotted anything worth taking off for, although he had squatted in beady anticipation a couple of times. Finally, he flapped down onto the middle of Ranch Road 54. In a minute, he was back on his perch, dragging the dried, stiffened carcass of a road-killed jackrabbit in one foot. Using everything he had to hang on to the

A clump of verbena adds color to
several small soapweed yuccas.

Arca Swiss 4 × 5. 90 mm Schneider lens.
Ektachrome.

Walking-stick cholla, small
soapweed yucca, prickly pear, and
rabbit brush on the high desert plateau.

Arca Swiss 4 × 5, 210 mm Schneider lens.
Ektachrome.

37

pole with his free talons, the owl bent and hooked his beak into the leathery carrion. A flapping heave backward tore loose a tiny piece, and after an hour of bobbing and yanking, all that was left were the big hind feet. One went down in a particularly ambitious gulp, but the second one landed crosswise in his crop and had to be flipped back up for another attempt on a different trajectory. This casual repacking is characteristic of the swallowing maneuvers that hawks and owls often go through in downing large prey, for swallowing is to them a much less final act than it is to a mammal. Their big neck pouch, or gorge, is not sealed away behind sphincters like a mammal's stomach, and little digestion goes on there. In some ways, it functions like a chipmunk's flexible cheeks, and, like the rodent's pouches, it may need to be repacked several times to fit everything in most compactly. Around the gorge is a net of smooth muscles which operate like a trash compacter. Small bones and soft tissue are squeezed from the chunks of mouse or rabbit gulped down in feeding and pass on down the gullet into the owl's stomach, while the teeth, hair, and claws of its prey are molded into a solid oval casting, not quite the size of a Ping-Pong ball in large birds, which is hiccupped out of the beak a few hours after the rodent went down. Dozens of these flaky gray castings were clumped beneath this bird's utility pole—apparently a long-time roost—along with the splatters of its whitewash droppings. Although casting is a daily occurrence for them, owls always look even more startled than usual when they burp up one of these plugs, and they eye the compressed little rodent mummies suspiciously, as if they might rehydrate and scurry away.

Four miles down the western scarp, another pair of great horned owls lives in the narrow road cut through Guadalupe Pass, periodically painting the cliffs below the best roosts with their mutes and hooting echoes to each other off the rock walls nearly every night. I have never seen them feeding, but they often perch along the white rims above the highway there and peer down at the tractor trailers groaning up the grade.

Above me, this morning's redtail finds a thermal and, circling within its swelling column of warm air, is drawn upward. The land seems awfully barren to have supplied a ground squirrel or cottontail in the few minutes since sunup, but around her throat a ruff of feathers like a russet ascot puffs out above the trim breast: her crop is full, so she is not hunting, just going for a ride, and has plenty of time to check out anything unusual down below among the familiar clumps of sage and cactus dotting her territory. She has seen all she wants now, though, and keels over into a tighter spiral as she climbs into the sun. As her outline shrinks to a speck no larger than the transcontinental jets overhead, I realize that she is also an aircraft. With passengers. Planktonic macrobes of grass and leaves still flourish in the innards of the rodents she carries tucked away in her crop. She needs them to survive. Besides the muscle and bone of her kills, she is also dependent on the intestinal flora of her prey to complete her own digestion, and she gains access to the vitamins and enzymes of green plants only by appropriating the undigested meals of her vegetarian victims. Carrying this cargo of kidnapped plant plankton, and almost beyond my sight now, she reaches the top of the escarpment and silently slides over the rim for a look around the bowl.

New Mexico agave, in life and in death.
Arca Swiss 4 × 5. 210 mm Schneider lens. Ektachrome.

The softness of old-man's-beard
contrasted against the sharp outline
of datil yucca.
Arca Swiss 4 × 5. 90 mm Schneider lens.
Ektachrome.

Claret-cup cactus in full flower.
Arca Swiss 4 × 5. 210 mm Schneider lens.
Ektachrome.

A fallen ponderosa pine with its
main trunk rotted away and the
more resistant limbs left in place.
Arca Swiss 4 × 5. 90 mm Schneider lens.
Ektachrome.

A sotol framed by massive limestone
boulders in South McKittrick
Canyon.
Arca Swiss 4 × 5. 90 mm Schneider lens.
Ektachrome.

Salt cedar against convoluted
limestone in Bone Canyon.
Arca Swiss 4 × 5. 210 mm Schneider lens.
Ektachrome.

Upper South McKittrick Canyon.
Arca Swiss 4 × 5. 90 mm Schneider lens.
Ektachrome.

3

April 16, 1968

Elk: Two bulls in velvet. Elk Canyon—out on horseback. Rode up to 30 feet of them. Saw them sleeping—only one got up and looked. They see me a million times a year and just let me ride through.

—R. REISCH
GUADALUPE MOUNTAINS NATIONAL PARK
WILDLIFE FILE: MAMMALS

FIVE YEARS before Douglas Lawson stumbled upon his pterosaur humerus in West Texas, Edward Lanning and Thomas Patterson found, at Cerro Chiveteros, in Peru, human artifacts more than 22,000 years old. They are the earliest exactly dated evidence of man in the New World. The villagers who chipped these stones were descendants of neolithic big-game hunters from northern Asia who passed through an ice-free corridor of newly exposed sea floor that lay to the north of the glaciers covering the Alaskan high country, and followed their imperial mammoth prey down into the central great plains. Since the hunters were not in any particular hurry to get to Peru, their original crossing could have been as much as 100,000 years ago. Similar spearheads have been turned up all over the Southwest. One of them, a folsom point, was found in Hermit Cave, in the Guadalupe's Last Chance Canyon, by E. B. Howard during the summer of 1933. It was buried amid the remnants of a basket-maker culture whose wicker cases were dated, by carbon-14 burning, at 12,000 years of age. Man had already spent more than three quarters of his present stay in the New World when someone dropped that spearpoint in Hermit Cave.

He was not an Indian, nor was he part of the earlier Clovis culture of the Trans-Pecos plains, which was a simpler society of big-game hunters who preyed on the most formidable mammals the continent ever held. Imperial mammoths loomed twelve feet at the shoulder, while both kinds of Pleistocene bison, as heavily built as stock-show Brangus, stood seven feet, with long curving horns. Ground sloths were twice the size of grizzlies. The men who killed them did so up close, with short spears and hand axes. During the 1950's, when the Clovis culture was first described, it seemed reasonable to assume that any hunter willing to tangle this intimately with even a stranded imperial mammoth had to be a physical viking. A series of *National Geograph-*

Bull elk (*Cervus canadensis*)

ic's "artist's concept" paintings of their imagined struggles furthered the impression. The skeletons of Clovis hunters don't bear this out, however; the people were short and looked like Eskimos. They also lived like them. Until the middle of the twentieth century, Eskimos maintained a hunting culture remarkably similar to that of stone-age man, killing big marine mammals, whales, and walruses at close range with the same throwing-stick weaponry that their inland counterparts used on the Pleistocene plains against mammoths and bison. It was a risky, indulgent survival strategy, geared to times of plenty. The Arctic Sea continued to supply plentiful large mammal prey until modern times, but, as the western plains dried out, the land no longer offered a sufficiently rich environment to maintain its early hunting cultures—completely dependent as they were on vast herds of large, slow-moving mammals that could be followed on foot—and big-game hunting became obsolete there ten thousand years ago.

For all the valor of its hunters, the Clovis culture was nevertheless a fragile one. Seldom able to corner their prey in open country, and limited by the short range of their spear-throwing sticks, the hunters were tied, for the most part, to well-watered valleys where the game would come to them. The valleys had to have ridges, for spotting the herds from a distance, and some sort of topographic trap—cliffs over which the bison could be stampeded, or bogs in which the mammoths could be mired. It was a luxury the society could not afford. If the game did not come, or grew wary of the traps after a few seasons, the hunters had to move on—and such sites were hard to find.

As the Pleistocene drew to a close, the biggest animals also found things tough on the drying prairie. Ground sloths, concentrated in the strips of woodland along rivers and around the waterholes, were the easiest kills for the newly arrived Arctic hunters, but they were as slow at reproduction as they were at everything else and were soon too scarce to rely on as game. Remnants of the wetland mammoth herds that fed in marshes stretching from the Gulf Coast to the Rockies retreated to the mountain forests to feed on conifer branches. By 9000 B.C., they had vanished from the Southwest. Bad weather had begun, and the heavy spears and axes that the Clovis hunters used to dispatch stranded elephants in the era of teeming herds became obsolete on the hard-soil prairies of pronghorns and the newly evolved modern bison—trimmed down to the limits of leaner pastures where waterholes lay a hundred miles apart and the herds moved opportunistically with the seasons, following the rain.

In the Guadalupe Mountains, archaeological sites have been systematically examined only since 1970, mainly by Paul and Susanna Katz, from the University of Texas. There are a great many of these sites, especially in the high country. Human artifacts have been found at the head of South McKittrick Canyon, in the Dog Canyon–Devil's Den area, along Blue Ridge, and near Pine Spring. Most of the artifacts belong to later, hunter-gatherer mountain tribes living in harder times than did the Clovis cultures of the plains. Agriculture was still unknown, and the high country was probably inhabited only during the summer by nomadic bands from several Paleo-Indian societies, now identified by the different types of wicker baskets each group used for gathering sotol roots. Besides their stone choppers and scrapers, they left midden rings which, toward the end of the last transitional cultures, are indistinguishable from those of modern Apaches. They also left pictures in Pine Spring Canyon. Twenty black pictographs remain on an overhanging rock face on the canyon's east wall, just north of the Shumard Peak fork. Eight are human figures, one is a circle with radiating lines like a kindergarten sun, and one is a long-horned sheep. Nothing else is known about them.

Eight thousand years ago, the real drought began: a massive continentwide altithermal lasting two millennia. By its end, the stone-age hunters were gone, and, in their place on the plains and in the mountains, were Indians. They were still nomadic hunter-gatherers, but they had a whole new weapons technology. After a half-million years of heavy choppers, axes, and spearheads, the crafting of stone tools had reached the level of refinement that allowed men to make tiny, cutting-edged projectile points light enough to be shot from a bow. The throwing stick that hurled the lances of the Clovis hunters was replaced with a better form of missile launcher.

But weapons development was the least important aspect of the Indians' hard-times technology. Gathering was far more important than hunting to the early Apache. They were a bad-weather tribe that came to the Guadalupes only recently—some six hundred years ago—into an arid habitat left vacant by a succession of previous Indian societies driven out by drought. Like Bedouins and Bushmen, Apaches were far from being the simple primitives they seemed to the first Europeans. Their culture was the result of five thousand years of adaptation to the narrow certainties of desert life, where relying on game as a primary food source was just too risky a strategy. Although they hunted bison on the plains during the calving season, when the herds were less mobile, and shot mule deer around the mountain springs in the cooler months, the Apaches' staff of life was cactus.

Agriculture in most of the Chihuahuan Desert was impossible, but Apache, Papagos, and other arid-country tribes were able to make use of equally stable, if less plentiful, food sources by harvesting the native desert plants. The stalks of sotol (*Dasylirion leiophyllum*) and various kinds of yucca were roasted, and their flowers and fruit eaten as snacks. The agave was even better. This desert-living *Amaryllis* lily thrives throughout the Southwest in arid country where cacti are the only other large plants, and its life cycle is perfect for human exploitation. For as many as twenty years, these smaller versions of the century plant grow conservatively, storing food in a central root crown surrounded by a cluster of armored leaves. They are preparing for a final reproductive fling. When enough energy has been stored, the agave sends up from its crown, in a matter of days, a huge priapic bloom stalk, as much as five inches thick and fifteen feet high. Even a little agave that could fit inside a washtub may produce a stalk of this size, capped by a flamboyant, two-foot cluster of yellow blossoms. Then the exhausted plant dies. The trick is to catch an agave just before it spends itself in this floral spree and appropriate the starches concentrated in its heart root. Apaches had the trick down pat.

The root crowns could be stored in baskets for months, since they did not spoil, and when a large enough inventory had been accumulated, all the heart roots were baked at once, directly on the coals of big, open pits lined with rocks banked around burning logs. More rocks placed over the dug-out centers made the pits into ovens, some of which were in use for generations, growing larger each time a new batch of coals was started over the floor of last season's roofing stones. The pits are called midden rings now, and they are found throughout the mountains where, because of their obviously man-made origin, they are a favorite haunt of neophyte arrowhead hunters, who never find projectile points in the old ovens.

Agave was the Mescalero's buffalo. Besides the carbohydrates of its heart root, the plant's fibrous leaves provided the Apache with thread, twine, and even needles from the horny tips. Pulped, they made soap. The flowers were eaten raw, and the seeds, along with acorns and piñon nuts, were ground into meal. The sap was fermented to make mescal, or pulque, which is still popular in Mexico. Refined, it is tequila. (For ceremonial occasions, mescal was spiked with a ground condiment of pulverized mountain laurel [*Sophora secundiflora*] beans, which gave it a hallucinogenic kick. The high was often terminal, however, since the beans from this legume—misleadingly called a laurel—are extremely toxic. After the 1880's, however, Apache medicine men, along with Indian cultures throughout the West, were caught up in the ghost dance religion and switched to the safer hallucinogen of the peyote cactus, making the same pilgrimages into Mexico for the buttons that their descendants follow today.)

Earthen jugs of mescal, as well as large batches of baked agave bread, jerky, and hides, were cached for lean times in tough, light baskets framed with the stiff stalks of bear grass and bound with yucca fibers. Except for dried jerky, most other food supplies were too heavy to be carried with the tribe when it moved—which was almost constantly—because the Apache were still afoot. The first European to see them was probably Antonio de Espejo, who encountered a small band of Mescalero on the prairie just east of the Guadalupe range, on August 7, 1583. They were heading for the mountains after a season preying on the calving buffalo. The dried meat and all their possessions were carried on small travois, pulled by dogs.

There had been native American horses, *Equus conversidens*, living on the great plains from central Mexico to Alberta since the Pliocene, but the Apache never saw them, and the early Paleo-Indian hunters thought of horses only as game, driving the animals into ravines and

spearing them for food. By the end of the Pleistocene, they were extinct
in North America, and the Comanche, Blackfoot, and Sioux evolved as
pedestrian predators, trotting behind the bison herds like lobos, living
mostly off the calves and stragglers.

Eight thousand years later, the first modern horses to set hoof in
the New World came ashore at Vera Cruz, in 1519, initiating both the
culmination of plains Indian culture as a brilliant equestrian society and
its ultimate downfall at the hands of the U.S. mounted cavalry. There
were fifteen mares, a stallion, and a new colt born on shipboard, all of
Moorish ancestry. Reinforced by additional shipments from Spain, they
flourished in Mexican pastures so well that Coronado, who departed
from Vera Cruz in 1540 to search as far north as Kansas for the golden
cities of Cíbolo, was able to muster five hundred mounted men and a
thousand extra horses. The Indians got only a few of the Spaniards, but
nearly a third of their horses.

By 1680, mounted Mescalero from the Guadalupe range were raiding the little settlement at El Paso del Norte, a hundred miles, or two
days' ride, to the west. Suddenly, tribes which had always been limited
to hunting grounds that their weakest members might reach on foot
could set up base camps and send scouting parties ranging hundreds of
miles over the prairie. Plunder was possible on a scale never possible
before, and raiding became a way of life for the Apache. Like the mammal communities which preceded them, the tribes divided into predator
and prey. For this balance to work, there could be only a few predators,
however, and the entire Apache nation never had more than 3,500 people. At its peak, the tribe could field only about 700 warriors. The plains
Navaho and nearby badlands Pueblo—five to seven times more numerous—were the first prey for Mescalero raiders from the Guadalupes,
as early as 1630. But Apache dominance on the prairie was short, and by
the turn of the century, Comanche horsemen from the llano estacado
dominated the grassland below the mountains. Breeders of horses, the
Mescalero called them, and their cavalry was strong enough to force
the Apache off the plains, splitting the culture into three tribes. Like
bighorn sheep, grizzlies, and elk, pushed from the prairie into the
mountains by later settlers, the Apache separated into small groups and
retreated into broken country where Comanche horsemen were less
effective. The Jicarillo became semisedentary residents of the southern
Rocky Mountains around Santa Fe, the Lipan Apache moved south and
east into the canyon country of the Edwards Plateau, and the Mescalero
and Chiricahua drew back into the Guadalupe and Sierra Blanca uplands where, for nearly two centuries, they raided their plains neighbors
and dodged the cavalry thrusts of both the Comanche and the U.S.
Army.

By the 1870's, however, their strategy had begun to fail. Federal
troops could still barely negotiate the canyon country when Maj. Albert
Morrow left Fort Quitman to eradicate the remaining Mescalero from
the Guadalupes, although the soldiers were too numerous and well
armed to fear direct attack. Their major problem was the terrain. In

league with another detachment from Fort Davis, under Lt. Gustavus Valois, the company of 150 men pressed up McKittrick Canyon and promptly became lost. Morrow wrote in his journal:

> The guides knew nothing of the country we were now in, but
> [I] again took up the trail and after marching four or five
> hours found myself back in the camp of the night before. In
> this march we passed about two hundred recently occupied
> lodges. . . . Our guides, although the best in the country,
> were completely baffled by the multiplicity of trails running
> in every direction, crossing and retracing. They finally suc-
> ceeded in finding a trail leading down what appeared to be
> an impassable ravine; the horses and pack mules had to be
> lifted over the rocks. One or two fell into crevices and could
> not be extricated. Toward evening we came across a ran-
> cheria of 75 lodges which the Indians abandoned at our
> approach leaving a large amount of mezcal bread, about two
> hundred gallons of an intoxicating beverage brewed from the
> maguey, and other commissary supplies, and a great number
> of hides, robes, and all sorts of utensils and furniture pertain-
> ing to an Indian village.*

In spite of their initial difficulties, the cavalry rapidly devastated the Mescalero, however. With their own predatory raids severely curtailed by federal troops, the tribe had once more been reduced to a subsistence-level culture whose material base was too narrow to sustain the systematic search-and-destroy warfare of Morrow, Valois, and the commander of the Manzanita Springs massacre, Lt. Howard Cushing. Cushing's raid occurred at the only waterhole east of the mountains, where the trickle from an aquifer spring collects in a swampy meadow just above the plains. The path to Manzanita Springs runs along the base of the eastern scarps, and in the evening cold gusts of wind slam down from the bluffs, flattening the buffalo grass and making us lean forward, into the waves. I pause at the old Mescalero encampment, but Allender, whose interests lie entirely in the present, forges on past. "Crazy bastard," he mutters. I presume he means Cushing. In the gale, I have to hold onto the plaque describing the attack in order to read it.

> Manzanita Springs
> Here on December 30, 1869, Lt. Howard B. Cushing com-
> manded his troop of the U.S. 3rd Cavalry in a bloody raid on
> a large rancheria, an Apache Indian village. His reputation
> was that of the most daring, gallant and reckless Indian
> fighter in the early West. Although there had been other at-
> tacks launched against the Apaches of these mountains,

*Letter of Major Albert Morrow to Acting Assistant Adjutant General, Subdistrict of the Presidio, June 1, 1870, in William H. Leckie, *Buffalo Soldiers: A Narrative of the Negro Cavalry in the West* (Norman: University of Oklahoma Press, 1970), p. 92.

none left such a vivid account as Lt. Cushing's report of relentless pursuit and destruction of a rancheria's material culture. The Mescalero Apache made the Guadalupe Mountains their home for over 300 years gathering mescal (agave) for food and raiding settlements . . . a cultural business for survival, not glory. When military protection of the increasing numbers of settlers threatened this way of life in the mid-1800's, these mountains became an essential Apache sanctuary. This refuge was invaded when, from behind the boulders on the lower slopes, a fire of rifle shot signalled the start of Cushing's raid. "Abandoning everything but their ponies, they rapidly scaled the steep slopes in scattered parties, driving their stock ahead of them." Dead horses and mules rolled down the mountainside. "Keeping some of my men after the Indians, I put others to work to destroy the rancheria." They burned immense numbers of buffalo robes, tanned deer and antelope skins, 20,000 lbs. of prepared mescal, and 15,000 lbs. of jerked beef. Indian saddles were added to the flames in such large numbers they were not even counted. Twenty-five ""wigwams," clothing, bows and arrows, cooking utensils, and liquor were either burned or carried off. "By hard labor, a little after dark, the destruction was complete, . . ."

It was a tactic the Apache had not encountered in three hundred years of predation on other Indians and whites, and they crumbled under its relentless pressure. Within a decade, the army strikes became massacres, as infantry joined the cavalry in penetrating deeper into the Guadalupe sanctuaries, overwhelming the Mescalero's home villages.

Meanwhile, the Trans Pecos was beginning to boom. Longhorn cattle herds were being driven into the area for the first time, and the east-west trails through the passes were tramped into roads. By this time, the unregulated existence of wild Indians—barbaric to the Victorian consciousness— was more of a psychological affront to a nation selling itself on the dream of a new land in the West than a substantial military barrier to expansion, but the affront was enough to define Cushing as a gallant and reckless hero. He was only one of the first, however. After Gettysburg, large numbers of U.S. cavalry were suddenly available to root out the Apache, and for these young war-trained captains and lieutenants, it was a marvelous opportunity to make a name for themselves against, by this time, mostly fugitive adversaries. The Texas Rangers also got into the act.

The remnants of the Guadalupe Mescalero who escaped Cushing and Morrow spent the next ten years on the run, as outlaws. The widely scattered waterholes in the Trans-Pecos were rapidly becoming stage stops by this time, however, and the few that remained unfortified were perfect traps. The Mescalero knew this as well as the cavalry, but they had to have water; and on January 29, 1881, the band rode straight into

an ambush led by George Baylor and a company of Texas Rangers at Hueco Tanks, fifty miles beyond the salt flats and the only unoccupied waterhole between the Guadalupes and the Rio Grande. The only survivor was an infant, shot through the foot, whom Major Baylor carried back to El Paso, noting disdainfully that it screamed at loud noises or gunfire. Afterward, only Geronimo's band of New Mexico Chiricahua remained at large—the last American Indians to move, unsubdued, across their homeland. The group was tiny: sixteen warriors, twelve women, and the two old war chiefs, Geronimo and Náchez. Most people thought of them as criminals. The moral perspective of the eighties made no extracultural allowances: law breakers had to be punished, especially if they were well publicized. The press followed Geronimo as closely as the cavalry, playing on the romance of hunting down exotic renegades, and the suddenly notorious Chiricahua drew an overwhelming public response. Federal marshals, bounty hunters, eastern adventurers, and the U.S. Army all took up Geronimo's trail, while Gen. Nelson Miles sent five thousand federal troops, four hundred Apache scouts, and hundreds of Mexican soldiers after the little band. His companies could cover forty miles a day on fresh horses. The Chiricahua sometimes rode seventy miles, ranging across the Guadalupes between bases in Mexico and the Sierra Blanca. When their horses gave out, or were shot, they managed fifty miles in a day on foot, dog-trotting. But they could not do it indefinitely, and after eighteen months of intensive pursuit, the Indians ran out of supplies. On September 3, 1886, Geronimo and Náchez rode alone into General Miles' camp at Skeleton Canyon, New Mexico, and laid down their rifles. Five days later, they were on a heavily guarded troop train headed for Florida. Most of the other passengers were photographers and correspondents.

A view of El Capitan and the salt flats beyond as seen from the top of the eastern escarpment.
Nikon FE. 28 mm Nikor lens.
Kodachrome.

Michael Allender
© 1980

4

July 16, 1978

Lion killed new-born calf of #3 radio collared elk. Was killed at Dog Canyon designated campground just down the road from the Ranger Station. Calf elk neck broke, chewed on hindquarters, dragged down into brush and covered with twigs and leaves. Found by John Moody, Harry Steed.

—R. REISCH
GUADALUPE MOUNTAINS NATIONAL PARK
WILDLIFE FILE: MAMMALS

IN WINTER, the six hundred miles from Austin to the Guadalupe Mountains are particularly long, because we cover most of them at night. There is often ice on the high plains from Sonora west: a black, nearly invisible coating called (misleadingly) glare ice, which flips my pickup almost sideways for a white-knuckled instant three times during the drive. Along the miles of dark highway beyond the Devil's River, we see the true high plains drifters: porcupines. In Colorado, porcupines sometimes spend their entire lives in one thick clump of spruce, feeding from tree to tree, but in West Texas they are, incongruously, nomadic drifters like the buffalo. But much slower. The cantering, free-ranging coyotes are in reality tied to specific territories, and the pronghorns born on a ranch's north forty will die there. Not porcupines. These stout travelers spend their lives in search of the evergreen foliage of the deeper ravines, eating their way through the sparse junipers of most draws in a few weeks and then trudging out across the plains, looking for another haven. On the prairie, porcupines graze on the same forbs as deer, for only in winter do they need the richer forage of evergreen bark, although they prefer it all year. The first porcupine I ever saw was a road-kill near Amarillo. I stopped the car and got out, not believing what I had passed: a montane forest-dweller squashed on the prairie three hundred miles from the Rockies. The porcupine was only out of place on the highway, however. He had just come up out of one arm of the Palo Duro Canyon for a deliberate stroll across the sorghum fields to another of the canyon's branches when technological disaster in the form of the pickup truck overtook him.

Porcupines used to live all over the state. They vanished from most places only within the last forty years, not because they were hunted

Ringtail (*Bassariscus astutus*)

much or actively exterminated (in spite of their predilection for gnaw-
ing), but rather because they were simply too slow to get out of man's
way. They were hit by cars, harassed by dogs, and conked on the head as
they peered mildly out of the junipers growing in people's suburban
yards. The last pair in Central Texas live at the Natural Science Center
in Austin. I have usually finished cleaning the cage and gone for their
food before it occurs to them that an affront to their territory is in progress. By the time I get back with apples and cantaloupe, both Prickles
and Buckets are whurffling quiet snorts of rage. It takes them a long
time to get over this, even when they smell the fruit and begin the
methodical search that always leads, after fifteen laborious minutes, to
their food bowl. The high plains porcupines are similarly out of synch,
trudging through the icy grass verges of West Texas highways at four in
the morning, like severely disheveled hitchhikers. They turn their
heads to watch us fly past, and I rack my brain thinking of a way to give
them a lift.

Ordinarily, Michael and I pass through Pecos at dawn. It is over a
hundred miles, and a slow, two-and-a-half-hour drive, from there to the
mountains, but, from the five-foot elevation of the railroad crossing at
the edge of town, El Capitan and the eastern palisades are sharp on the
horizon. They could be ten feet high or three thousand because there
is no perspective to measure their size or distance across the empty
plains. On September 23, 1858, the first passenger carried by the Butterfield Overland Stage Company was Waterman Lily Ormsby, who corre-
sponded to his paper, the *New York Herald*: "From Pope's Camp, in the
bright moonlight, we could see the Guadalupe mountains, sixty miles
distant on the other side of the [Pecos] river, standing out in bold relief
against the clear sky . . ." As his stagecoach plugged along like a porcupine, up the steep eastern side of the mountains, Ormsby wrote:

> The Guadalupe peak loomed up before us all day in the most
> aggravating manner. It fairly seemed to be further off the
> more we travelled, so that I almost gave up in despair all
> hopes of reaching it. Our last eight or ten miles were along
> the foothills of the range, and I now confidently believed that
> we were within a mile or two, at the outside. But the road
> wound and crooked over the interminable hills for miles yet
> and we seemed to be no nearer than before. I could see the
> outline of the mountains plainly, and as I eagerly asked how
> far it was, Henry Skillman, the driver, laughingly told me it
> was just five miles yet, and we had better stop and give the
> animals a rest or they could never finish it.*

Before crossing the summit of the pass, Ormbsy spent the night at Pine
Spring Station, where his stage got a fresh team of horses for the climb.
Of the stables and inn that the Butterfield Company maintained there,

---

*Waterman Lily Ormsby, *The Butterfield Overland Mail*, ed. L. H. Wright and
J. M. Bynum (San Marino, Calif.: Huntington Library, 1942), p. ix.

all that remains now are rows of flat red rocks that mark the founda-
tions of the old walls. The ditch that channeled water down from Pine
Spring, a mile up in the canyon, has been eroded away for a long time,
and its bed is overgrown with cholla, lechuguilla, and rabbit brush.

If the mountains are solid white at Pecos, we know the road will be
closed beyond the next intersection, at Orla; but closed out here means
just a sign stuck on a sawhorse. The ranch trucks swing on past, and so
do we. Two hours later, coming in to Signal Peak camp over sixty miles
of unmarked snowy roads gives us the feeling of making the Malemute
Saloon after a long mush. One of the trailers in the camp is to be our
home. Ranger Joe Vinson leaves his door open to us, even when he is
away. On his table, a thick tract called *A Basis for Facility Development
at Guadalupe Mountains National Park*—which everyone calls the
Master Plan—blueprints the facility's future. Michael flips absently
through the pages for awhile, until one of the proposals seizes his
attention.

A view westward from the Williams
homestead below Bone Canyon.
Nikon FE. 55 mm micro Nikor lens.
Kodachrome

"The sons of bitches want to build a three-thousand-foot-long chairlift up Guadalupe Peak!" The project anticipates for Allender the negation of everything he has been putting himself through: the cost of the high vistas has always been a steep, two-thousand-foot climb, and the prospect of an easily accessible overlook cheapens his effort to get photographs for which no one else has yet been willing to pay the price. The roar of incipient freeways cuts through the silence.

It's hard for me to be threatened by the Master Plan at this point, however. There is still a lot of Texas west of the Pecos left to be domesticated, and the Guadalupe range is right in the emptiest part of it. Established only since 1972, the park is so new that there is nothing much here yet. The main ranger station, a small frame house, is its only building, except for some maintenance sheds, on the eastern side of the mountains, while, ten miles away, on the far side of Guadalupe Pass, Vinson's trailer is one of twelve nearly identical beige boxes clustered just off the highway below Signal Peak promontory. The rangers' names are cut into small boards that hang by their doors. Except for an El Paso Gas Company pumping station just up the road, Signal Peak Housing Area is the only settlement between El Paso, a hundred miles to the west, and Whites City, New Mexico, sixty-five miles eastward. There is practically nothing in between but rugged brown mountains. Almost all the rangers and staff (about forty-five people) live here, in the midst of one of the widest open spaces left in the United States, on a tiny, dusty tract that would be lost in the parking lot of a small-town Holiday Inn. Tonight, there are a dozen of us packed into Vinson's living room. The atmosphere is Mayberry R.F.D.

Everyone wants to hear about Michael's latest expedition, but what has really drawn the big crowd is his promise, last trip, to bring some drawings when he returned. Happy to house a celebrity in their midst, Caroline Wilson—Guadalupe Mountains National Park's interpretive naturalist—who is resplendent in turquoise and an embroidered Navaho dress, persuades Michael to bring in his pictures: mule deer, a cougar, mallards jumping into flight from the reed beds. He is the kind of artist the rangers respond to. Every one of them is here because he or she cherishes the stark peaks and their wildlife, and Michael has been driving twelve hundred round-trip miles every few weeks to share it. Because they are patient, careful people beneath their repartee, they appreciate Michael's painstaking craftsmanship. I, in turn, am struck by the singular way in which everyone looks directly at me while I talk and waits for me to say all I want, which is usually too much. Even that is all right. There is plenty of time, with no need for the urban conversational hustle of finishing another's sentence or staring off impatiently to hurry a tedious exchange to conclusion.

Dee and Gaylord Scott decide to buy a mule deer print—the artifice of a month at the drawing board—and Michael awkwardly accepts their money. She is blonde, efficient, a park ranger. He is the law (Texas Highway Patrol) west of the Pecos and east of El Paso along U.S. 180. Gaylord is jovial and not inclined to take himself seriously. He tells us he mainly gives warning citations to speeders, but once in awhile he has more interesting work, like escorting motorcycle gangs—Banditos from Houston, Angels from Los Angeles—when they pass through his territory.

The Scotts are a little uneasy about buying one of Michael's drawings. He is the only artist they know.

"How long you been an . . . " Scott begins. "Been doing all this drawing?"

Allender scuffles his feet, equally uncomfortable with "artist." "About four years."

Michael became an artist by outlining precise anatomies of *Corridorus* catfish for the Smithsonian Institution, and his scientific entry into the field makes it easier for him to accept being an artist. For his audience, Michael elaborates. It is one of his favorite stories. As a graduate student, scrounging for himself and the four coyote pups, he was asked by another student to finish detailing a fish she was drawing for the National Museum's structural anatomy collection. He had never drawn before, but she was leaving, the work paid $150, and he figured it couldn't take more than a few hours. After a week spent hunched over the deteriorating two-inch catfish, the drawing was finished, and Allender had a job with the Smithsonian. "If I hadn't done that blasted minnow," he tells the group, "I'd be a ranger now." They nod in sympathy.

A few travelers use the parking lot at Pine Spring as a roadside stopover for their motor campers year round, but during the winter we are often the only outside visitors beyond the pavement in all of the park's 120 square miles. There are not many new faces then, and the rangers appreciate Allender's efforts to get here almost as much as they do his intrepid backpacking forays. The only real driving hazards are icy roads and the wind shear through the pass. Northers sweeping down across the plains hit the long wall of the western Guadalupe scarps, building intense pneumatic pressure that swells until the backrising current boils up over the high rim, exploding the steady alpine wind at eight thousand feet to over a hundred miles per hour in seconds. When this happens, the dead air pockets beyond the eastern cliffs add their enormous suction, and the sudden ebb and flow pulls gusts back and forth like rip tides through the narrow break in the mountains between El Capitan and the Delaware ridges to the south. Because the gap makes three right-angled bends, the wind can almost blow in both directions at the same time. The two orange windsocks that mark the opposite ends of the gorge, not quite three miles apart, are frequently blown out rigid from their pylons, downwind tips pointing directly toward each other. With the steering wheel angled far into one of these currents, it is easy, in a matter of a hundred feet, to have crossed the shear line, entered the opposite fifty-mile-per-hour wind stream—and been blown across the oncoming traffic lane onto the opposite shoulder. Vinson doesn't have much trouble with his 750 Suzuki, surprisingly, but has gotten knocked off the road a couple of times in his pickup.

Maple leaf and saw grass in
McKittrick Canyon.
Arca Swiss 4 × 5. 210 mm Schneider lens.
Ektachrome.

Water striders and dead moths
floating in a pool over decaying leaves.
Arca Swiss 4 × 5. 210 mm Schneider lens.
Ektachrome.

Big Wind stories are a conversational staple. The U.S. Meteorological Service routinely records hurricane-force winds in the pass itself, and everyone loves to tell about the automatic weather station high on Guadalupe Peak which beamed down signals measuring the highest wind velocity it was designed to record—170 miles per hour. Then the station blew away.

Michael swears that his van, laden with twenty-five extra gallons of fuel, nearly blew over one night, scaring him so much he considered sleeping outside in a ditch. Allender is probably the only person in the world from whom I'd believe that story, and it sounds dubious even from him. House trailers are overturned here all the time, but they seem more rickety to me than 6,500 solid pounds of Ford Econoline. I did see Michael and his big Sherpa pack blown into McKittrick Creek, however. He stepped off one stone, surefootedly aiming for the next rock just as a particularly strong gust hit him, and set his foot down in waist-deep water three feet downwind an instant later.

Mainly, though, the wind just wears you down. Out on the prairie, it is as steady as a tropic trade, but about twice as strong. In the canyons, there are nice periods of dead calm, especially in mid-afternoon, but by dusk the cliffs begin to shed their afternoon heat, and the resulting convection rolls billows of cold air down the canyons like flash-flood waves. At the mouth of McKittrick, the little aluminum caravan used as a portable ranger station is attached to the parking lot with four thick turnbuckled guy wires. Even in blustery weather, this seemed silly to me until I found the frazzled cables which used to anchor a similar, station-wagon-sized trailer that now lies upturned, a hundred yards downwind of a nearby canyon.

Above Guadalupe Pass, the winds are even heavier, and, because their eddies and downdrafts are both invisible and completely unpredictable, the peaks are a hazardous area for light planes. Guadalupe Park rangers hauled out the carcass of a helicopter last fall, and the high country hides scores of previous crashes. (American Airlines has stuck a shiny silver monument honoring the early mail pilots downed by these winds on top of Guadalupe Peak, on the highest point in the state, 8,751 feet, but it is as ugly as the wrecks it memorializes.) For light planes in trouble over the mountains, there is only one place to land, but it is a good one, if they can clear the western escarpment. Eighteen miles beyond is the graded gravel airstrip of the U.S. Weather Service office; but three thousand feet below the cliffs, and only a half dozen glide-path miles away, are the broad expanses of the dry salt lakes. They look like runways from the air, and, although they are not nearly as smooth, planes have made it in on a wing and a prayer, spewing salt as they touched down. One of these was a Piper Apache twin that took me in for a bumpy forced landing there in December of 1960.

McKittrick Creek.
Arca Swiss 4 × 5. 210 mm Schneider lens.
Ektachrome.

Looking north across the top of the
Guadalupe Mountains: January, six
inches of new snow, − 5 °F.
Arca Swiss 4 × 5. 210 mm Schneider lens.
Ektachrome.

The ruins of the Butterfield Stage
depot framed against El Capitan in
mid-winter.
Arca Swiss 4 × 5. 90 mm Schneider lens.
Ektachrome.

Michael Allender
'80

5

June 3, 1977

Prairie Falcon. Pair of falcons flying after violet-green swallows (just playing) under Bartlett Peak. Lloyds ledge area 10:10 A.M.

—CHIHUAHUAN DESERT RESEARCH INSTITUTE,
ALPINE, TEXAS
GUADALUPE MOUNTAINS NATIONAL PARK
WILDLIFE FILE: BIRDS

A T PINE SPRINGS CAMPGROUND, the garbage can lids are weighted with thick cement discs. This makes it hard to get rid of trash, but it doesn't stop the raccoons At night, I hear them working their way down the row, clanging into can after can, and I remember Diamond Lake, Oregon, where the trash barrels are fifty-gallon drums, sealed with three latches and chained to concrete slabs. This is to prevent black bears from rolling the barrels away and bouncing them down hills until they break open on stumps and logs. There are bears here, too, but there are no campground raiders among them. Until recently, they were heavily hunted, and those that survived are still very afraid of people.

Except for occasional forays down into McKittrick Canyon, the bears remain in the high country, and the loud crunching footsteps that skirt my sleeping bag turn out to be only mule deer. They are extremely bold, however. From upwind, they walk right up to me, standing in the dark, whuffling and casting their big donkey ears forward until my scent from five feet away tells them I am not the other deer they anticipated. The salt they come for is a residue of the tepid Permian Sea which remained liquid, buried three-quarters of a mile below the surface here, until a Texaco drilling crew tapped into it in 1967 and pumped the ancient ocean water out of the core casing and onto the flat ground surrounding their rig. Texaco and Standard Oil, which drilled another research hole at the mouth of McKittrick Canyon, wanted to make sure, before they gave up their mineral rights to the new park, that there were no minerals of any value to give up. Capped and sealed now, the well is marked only by a large beige box over its old casing in the middle of Pine Spring parking lot; but the Permian salt it decanted is still crusted

Peregrine falcon (*Falco peregrinus*)

70

among the rocks, and mule deer traipse among the campers nightly to scoop it out with their long pink tongues.

These Pine Spring residents seldom resort to full flight, preferring to walk sedately out of the path of hikers. When they are really startled, though, mule deer bound away in stiff-legged pogo-stick hops like horizontal kangaroos. The cartoon skunk Pepe le Peu sproings along exactly like a fleeing mule deer. They nearly always run uphill, for predators long ago weeded out the ones that ran down into the trap of narrow gulches and box canyons. That is where water and forage lie, but maneuvering room for escape is tight. Bounding uphill springs the animals out over the canyon rims onto the open mesas, where speed counts, and requires them to be much more heavily muscled than the gracile Central Texas white-tails. During the winter of 1978, Caroline Wilson spooked a large buck, whose only uphill option was an eighth of a mile of forty-five degree angled ice pack. He lunged up the incline in great bounds, but, just shy of the top, the entire slope collapsed in a minor avalanche, carrying him crashing far down into a canyon. Eventually, Caroline saw him paw free of the snowbank, shake, and trot off.

If mule deer love to run uphill, pronghorns are absolutely berserk about it. They are also determined to run into the wind; and if the wind and uphill do not lie in the same direction, it's a hard decision, but they usually choose to go uphill. Driving into the Guadalupes from El Paso, I spotted a small band of antelope grazing just north of the highway. Beyond them, the park road to Williams Ranch lay both upwind and on slightly higher ground. By the time the whistle blast from a transcontinental eighteen-wheeler had shot the herd into flight, I was parked midway along the road, my pickup in plain view. But that's no obstacle to a panicked pronghorn with the wind in his face and high ground ahead. The herd reached the fence and streamed through the barbed wire, a few does plunging between the strands, but most of them, and all the fawns, sliding under the bottom wire nose first, at full speed, like runners diving for home plate. Momentum intact, they were on their feet again instantly, stretching out into a full run, having barely broken stride. It was a beautiful, long-lasting frenzy of plunging black hooves and muzzles, white and tan flanks, and wide, terrified eyes. All except the herd buck. Rearguard of the twenty-odd animals, he balked at the fence, bucking, and then danced nervously along its length like a race horse, snorting at his consorts, whose white rumps were disappearing to the east. Thinking the truck might have scared him, I slowly backed away, but this only sent him flying back in the direction he had come. He ran parallel to the highway for a long time, and I was able to keep him in sight until dusk, using an 80x spotting scope. I saw him last just at dark, far out on the salt flats, fifteen miles from his band up in the Patterson foothills, loping about in long, aimless loops.

Like all plains-living ungulates, pronghorns are herd creatures who depend on the collective senses of their companions as multiple alarms to keep distant from predators—in this area, coyotes—and a solitary antelope, too large to hide, cannot maintain the level of vigilance he needs to survive. That night, as I dozed in my down bag, I again watched the fawn-and-white herd stream across the road; but the image of that confused, solitary buck whose life I had unraveled was much stronger.

The elk here are more stable, but you have to wait for them. As we sit in the old game blind at the edge of their swampy browsing meadows by Manzanita Springs, Michael is quiet, but he's not really waiting for the elk to show up; he's being nice to me by enduring this trial of his patience. Allender can get all the details he needs for his drawings from photographing captive animals or looking at other people's slides, and in his precious, hard-bought time in the mountains he is restless, gazing at the failing light.

All around us are the huge gouged prints the elk have left in the spring bank mud. They are not the indigenous Merriam's species, which were hunted out by the 1880's, but wapiti, exotics introduced from South Dakota. Ten years before the turn of the century, not only the Merriam's elk, but also the American elk, or wapiti, stood with the bison on the brink of extinction. Less than a hundred wapiti remained in the country, half of them in Yellowstone National Park, which had been set up in 1872 as the first national preserve in the United States. By 1900, the herd had doubled and, in an attempt to spread the odds for the elk's survival, 5 bulls and 9 cows were sent to the Wind Cave refuge in South Dakota, followed two years later by another 25 animals. But Wind Cave is a small sanctuary and the elk rapidly outstripped its available forage. To thin the second herd, which had mushroomed to 170 animals by 1928, roughly one-fourth of them were trapped and sent to Texas—a donation by Wind Cave to J. C. Hunter, Sr., and the Grisham-Hunter Corporation—as game animals.

Forty-seven of the badly frightened elk, inventoried at between $41.00 and $55.00 per head, left Wind Cave in April 1929, riding in a seventy-foot steel baggage car divided into six compartments in an attempt to keep the animals from shifting too much with the train's movement and crushing those on the downhill side. Even so, six of the smaller elk were trampled to death during the two-day trip. At Carlsbad, the survivors were transferred to trucks for the final leg of their journey to a pen at the mouth of McKittrick Canyon, where, just as they were being unloaded, five of them panicked and broke through the sides of their slatted cattle shoot, escaping into the barren plains below the eastern cliffs where no one thought they could survive. After a short acclimatization in the holding pen, the other thirty-six animals were released into the canyon, where water and foliage were abundant, although the elk preferred the arid montane forests beyond the rim and immediately clambered up out of McKittrick, never to return. Their descendants—over a hundred animals now—remain in the high country, despite the increasingly poor pasturage there. They are entirely dependent for their supply of water on a small, rain-fed earthen stock tank in the bowl. Although the pond has never been known to dry up completely, for much of the year the elk drink more mud than water,

and the calves are sometimes killed there by mountain lions ranging across the peaks. The five original escapees also survived—apparently knowing a good habitat when they saw one—and their offspring have established a small herd on the rolling plains just east of park headquarters. Hunter's line cabin up in the canyon now stands in a beautiful, but elkless, glen.

The plains band waters at Manzanita Springs, and most evenings they drift onto the adjacent marshy flats around dark. They are wary, but Allender has their number. As they approach, still an eighth of a mile distant, the elk raise their noses. They are alert, on the point of flight. Michael is equally tense and, spotting the herd, decides he can take no more of the confinement of the blind and slides from his perch on its log wall. I expect him to belly down behind the sparse lechugilla and begin a long stalk. Instead, he yells at them. "Hello, elk!" Michael sings out cheerfully, setting out on a diagonal past the group. The elk watch carefully for a minute. Then they begin to chew the grass that dangled motionless from their mouths in the moment before flight. A few minutes later, Michael reaches another trail, which approaches the spring in a long oblique loop and, talking softly, moseys casually down toward the water, thirty yards from the animals. All seven lower their heads to graze.

Far too alert to stalk, it turns out, the elk apparently don't mind an up-front approach, reminding me of wildebeests grazing confidently near well-fed Serengetti lions. The fears of most open-country ungulates are similarly tuned to suspicious or covert actions, and, since they are not hunted here, the elk are relatively tolerant of people as long as they can see what is going on. Michael talks to them just as a personal touch.

It seems to work. One October afternoon, I watch him coax a yellow-faced pocket gopher out of its burrow for a snack of cheese crumbs. The gopher is apprehensive but not really afraid, although he stays hidden, except for his twitching nose, behind the loose plug of sod that serves as his door. Making tentative nibbling motions with his big orange incisors, he inches forward, holding his earthen divot before him like a manhole cover. Clicking his tongue every few seconds, Michael is as calm as Dr. Welby, assuring the little animal that the Coopers hawks are all asleep way up in the canyons. The clicks are there to accustom the gopher to the sound so that he won't flinch when the shutter trips.

I remember seeing the same whimsy coupled with total professionalism years before. Harry Pederson made nature documentaries for Disney during the period when the studio still saw family entertainment from the *National Geographic* perspective and turned out films like *The Living Desert* and *The Vanishing Prairie*. Pederson and his sons, Tom and Chris, seemed perpetually charmed, first amazed to be paid at all for doing the neatest thing they could imagine and, second, astonished at themselves every time they got close enough to a shy creature to get the shots they needed. Their footage was crushed and stretched into procrustean scripts by the studio, but, for a long while,

A vertical limestone cliff reflected in a quiet pool in the upper reaches of South McKittrick Canyon.
Nikon FE. 28 mm Nikor lens.
Kodachrome.

the men retained their initial delight with whatever seal or clownfish filled their viewfinders.

The requirements of shooting staged scenes eventually asked too much, however, and the spell was broken. The Pedersons split up and became portrait photographers, but their early footage, run silent, free of the cartoon-animal characterizations of the studio soundtracks, is more than fine nature photography; it is also documentary of their elation at being the first to record, and often the first to see, the mating dances of pelagic birds, shrimp with their cleaning stations, or jawfish druids building their miniature stone circles. Michael shares both their empathy for wild creatures and the pioneer elation of being the first to carry a big format camera into the Guadalupe back country. His delight in this role fuels everything he does out here, although its responsibilities constantly imply a heavy pressure to perform.

Incongruous as it seems, the sky across the Guadalupes is full of jet trails, because the area is both a course coordinate, or course alteration, point for the transcontinental liners and a maneuver zone for the military jets from Fort Bliss' Biggs Field that criss-cross above and below the 747's. One of these fighters, its pilot spending free time to keep up his flight log, is playing over El Capitan one winter evening, cutting back and forth through the long plume of snow cloud that sometimes hangs from the face of the precipice. Allender has just bounded up an equally steep roadside bluff to get a photograph of the mist-framed peak at the moment when its daylight gray will glow brightest pink in the sunset. Wrestling with his tripod and camera, Michael notices the contrail scar across his previously pristine scene. He stops for about three seconds, aware of having driven thousands of miles and spent weeks waiting for the picture.

"You devil," he shouts, shaking his fists. The contrail is blowing away quickly, but the light is also going, and, as we stand there watching the white line fade against the rapidly darkening sky, it is about to be a strained moment. Michael looks down at his boots, wedged between cholla spines, yucca, and broken blocks of shale, and starts to explode. Then he thinks better of it. "You don't dare kick anything out in this country," he observes. On the way back to camp, one of the great horned owls that hoot and flap through the road cut below El Capitan settles for a moment on top of a bluff, silhouetted against a three-quarter moon. It is an arresting sight that will not come again, and the need to record it momentarily narrows Allender to a focused beam of furious intensity. There is no time to set up the big camera, though, and the Nikon is packed beneath a ton of gear. Ten seconds after this becomes evident, Michael is as serene as before, and we just enjoy the owls with our eyes and ears.

The brushy slag around the Pine Spring trailhead is crowded with the floppy white flowers of *Argemone platyceras*. These spiny bushes are appropriately called pricklepoppy or thistlepoppy, and each plant may carry a dozen or more blossoms. The altitude here is nearly six

Second water crossing in McKittrick Canyon.
Arca Swiss 4 × 5. 210 mm Schneider lens. Ektachrome.

thousand feet, so although it is dry, the flora is more montane than Chihuahuan, and the trails leading up into Pine and Bear Canyons are bordered with many variations of yellow and white flowers of the sunflower family. Because these plants are usually no more than two feet tall and alternate between yellow- and white-petaled forms, they are called desert daisy, wild daisy, and dwarf daisy. One of the prettiest is the plains blackfoot (*Melampodium leucanthum*), with its double layer of clean white petals and bright yellow centers.

Farther up the slopes, particularly on the sheltered western sides of both canyons, grows the pink paintbrush of the Guadalupes (*Castilleja sessiliflora*), a high-country version of the red Indian paintbrush common along East and Central Texas highways. It blooms from early summer until late in the fall, especially if the summer is a little wetter than usual. Like many paintbrushes, *sessiliflora* is parasitic on the roots of various grasses, relying on them for nutrients it is unable to produce by its own photosynthetic process. For some reason, most of the mountain wildflowers here share the paintbrushes' predominantly pink or red coloration, and many are found nowhere else in the state. The brilliant wood lily (*Lillium philadelphicum*) ordinarily lives in Canada and the northwestern United States and, like the royal beard-tongue (*Penstemon cardinalis*), is found this far south only in the Guadalupe cordillera, although a similar red stemon (*P. barbatus*) can be seen throughout the Trans-Pecos. Both penstemons—long, red flowers, whose throats are guarded by pouty upper and lower lips—begin flowering in early spring and have bloom periods which overlap that of the scarlet gilia (*Ipomopsis aggregata*) in late summer, when the two plants are easily confused, although the tubular throat of the scarlet gilia has a star-shaped opening.

Guadalupe Peak from Pine Top.
Arca Swiss 4 × 5. 210 mm Schneider lens.
Ektachrome.

Bull thistle silhouetted against cumulus clouds near El Capitan.
Nikon FE. 55 mm micro Nikor lens.
Kodachrome.

Hummingbirds are suckers for red, tubular flowers like these everywhere in the hemisphere, and the profusion of penstemons and gilias in the high canyons draws black-chinned and broad-tailed hummers in small, buzzing flocks that sometimes number ten or twelve birds. Rufous, blue-throated, and Anna's hummingbirds also occur here, and broad-bills and ruby-throats are occasionally seen. Because they follow the flowers in a clockwise circuit of seasonal travel across the Southwest, like fruit pickers moving with the ripening crops, most western hummingbird species show up here at one time or another during the growing season. This profusion of hummers is exceeded only in Central America and the Caribbean, for, although the little birds seem out of place in these barren desert mountains, the Guadalupes' enormous variation in altitude and moisture offers many more discrete floral microhabitats than the lushly foliaged lowlands of eastern Texas.

One of the broad-tails' nests, cut from a big-toothed maple in McKittrick Canyon for display at the visitor center, is woven out of spider webs and filaments of feathers, crusted with a camouflaging outer coat of lichens. The thimble cup within the shell seems too small for even these leprechauns, and, in fact, its size is a major problem for hummers. Like hawks, hummingbirds lay only two eggs, and, like them, only one of the babies ordinarily survives. Because there is so little room inside the marble-sized demitasse, as the young approach adult size, the weaker is almost always shouldered out of the nest, fully feathered, only a week or two before it can fly. This stunning waste of life prevails throughout the natural process, however, and emphasizes how alien its blank pragmatism is to human values. The finality of their juvenile competition may also be the reason why hummers are such feisty little birds: the more placid ones never fledged.

Another flower endemic to the Guadalupe canyons is the yellow chapline columbine (*Aquilegia chaplinei*), which may be found in bloom anytime from early spring to midfall in McKittrick Canyon but which is especially luxuriant in September. Apaches looked on the columbine as good medicine and boiled its roots as a treatment for bruises. Tea brewed from the plant was considered a good body toner, and the seeds were thought to be even stronger and prized as an aphrodisiac.

It is easy to tell mints—they have square stems. Texas has over a hundred different kinds, most of which are small and inconspicuous until one smells their crushed leaves underfoot, when it is too late for the mint. One species, the pink-flowered mountain sage mint (*Salvia summa*), had been found only in the shady canyons of the Guadalupes until recently, when a few plants were also discovered in southwestern New Mexico. The most common variation, however, are the various *monarda* horsemints, wild bergamot, and bee-balm, which have tall, lavender or yellow stalks of pungent flowers. Another aromatic mint, blooming from midsummer to late fall, is the rare canyon sage (*Salvia lycioides*). Its fine dark-blue flower stands out among the predominantly red high-country blooms and can sometimes be found above the springs in Guadalupe Canyon at around seven thousand feet.

Fire and ice blending on the face of
El Capitan early on a January morning.
Arca Swiss 4 × 5. 210 mm Schneider lens.
Ektachrome.

Michael Ollender
'80

6

July 7, 1970

McKittrick Canyon. . . . Two Mexicans on way to Hobbs from El Paso left male fawn (about 2 days old) at McKittrick Ranger Station. Mother presumed to have been killed. First evening fawn was fed whole milk from a plastic baby bottle. Fawn would not suck but would swallow occasionally when mouth filled with milk. Fawn was kept in pen next to metal shed for first five days. Morning of third day, began sucking. "Big 'un" was mixed with warm milk and fed three times a day. After five days, fawn had gained considerable strength and was turned loose in ranger station enclosure for three days. Fawn was then removed from enclosure and set free. Fawn continues to return to enclosure gate twice a day (morning and evening) where he is given a one-pint mixture of condensed milk and water. On July 10, he began eating mimosa leaves. On July 24, he began eating alfalfa in hay at horse pen. August 25—began eating acorns—small bowl of acorns given each feeding. September 10—lost spots and went into winter coat. September 15— began eating oats at horse pen.

—R. REISCH
GUADALUPE MOUNTAINS NATIONAL PARK
WILDLIFE FILE. MAMMALS

ALLENDER has been away on his circuit of art shows for months when I pull up, hours late, next to his white van, parked at the end of the last stretch of dirt road below Guadalupe Peak. It is a familiar oasis: the chuckwagon. The stove is lit and I can smell dinner. Then an apparition thrusts its head out the window. The gnarled hands and long leathery neck suggest a Galápagos tortoise costumed with glasses and a frizzy white beard. "Where you been, boy? I've had a long wait." Fixing me with a glittering eye worthy of the ancient mariner, the apparition whips a pair of long-nosed scissors, carved like a heron, out of a scabbard on his belt and begins to whittle away at a sheet of black paper. I have never seen a scissor scabbard before. In moments, the paper has become my silhouette—cut freehand, without a shadow.

The Wizard of the Scissors, as his card announces, is Paul Hoyt, a fellow exhibitor of Allender on the art circuit, who attached himself to Michael at the Roswell exhibition. He is more or less on the lam from his family, who live in the desert twenty miles from Truth or Con-

Mule deer (*Odocoileus hemionus*)

sequences, New Mexico. He says they have been giving him a hard time for being a hippie. He is also mad because he has left both his Bronchaids and his last joint of cannabis in his car at Pine Spring, where it ran out of ground clearance. Hoyt is to camp with us at Williams Ranch, midway back in the park at the base of the western escarpment, and climb Bone Canyon.

For nearly an hour, my pickup creeps and jounces along a pair of jumbled stone tracks cut through the sotols, yuccas, and agaves growing below the western cliffs. Besides juncos and a pair of white-necked ravens, the most prominent animals are burrowing owls. They live in holes which they share with bullsnakes, jackrabbits, striped skunks, and prairie rattlers, among others. No one knows whether any symbiotic partnerships are involved, but a simpler and more likely explanation is that none of these creatures is forceful enough to drive the others out. The snakes and the owls both eat mainly white-footed and pocket mice, but the snakes also eat baby owls when they find them unguarded, and the owls, in their turn, have been seen with small rattlers dangling from their beaks. The most dangerous animal in the Trans-Pecos also lives in these stony foothills. The Mojave rattler can be told from prairie rattlers and diamondbacks only by the upper white eye-stripe that curves above the rear corner of its mouth and by the very wide white bands that alternate with much narrower black rings around its tail. It is important to be able to distinguish Mojave rattlers because they are ten to fifteen times as deadly as even the large diamondback. They are the only North American serpents, other than the coral snakes, to carry a substantially neurotoxic venom. A close relative of the similarly neurotoxic-venomed Brazilian and Central American rattlers, including *Crotalus durissis terrificus*, whose potency lives up to its name, the Mojave also carries a lot more venom than a coral snake. Dr. Findlay Russell, who has treated more of their bites than anyone else, reports only two results: the majority of cases, in which no envenomation occurred, and fatalities. Fortunately, they are very rare, and even herpetologists (who rate them a real find) have only turned up a handful here during the past decade.

Burrowing owls do not tangle with even baby Mojaves, although the nestlings do a good job of buzzing like rattlers at the first vibration of footsteps near their den. This is a great protective ruse for the owls, but it has furthered the myth of subterranean harmony between snakes and owls. Although burrowing owls are not as exclusively nocturnal as most, they still squint a lot in the bright sunshine and look nearly as sleepy as other owls during the day. They are seen most often just before sunset, though, when they emerge to stand around on long yellow legs near the mounds marking the mouths of their burrows. They appear to have no tails, which, combined with their rapid waddle, makes them look like beige, short-beaked desert penguins. By late afternoon they are restless with hunger and sometimes fly up to perch in the creosote bushes (which are really too spindly to support them) and hang there, flapping unsteadily. The owls are waiting until full dark brings the silky pocket mice up from their daytime bedrooms. Merriam's kangaroo rats emerge about the same time. They are the ultimate reflex artists among rodents and are so quick on the jump that they usually don't even bother to hide when they feed in the open. For predators, catching one is like a man grabbing a housefly, and the owls seldom even try for them. Coyotes have a higher frustration tolerance, however, and can sometimes nab kangaroo rats by setting up a couple of catcher animals, who get at least a shot at the ricocheting rats set off by the flusher coyote.

As we creak along the foot of the western palisade, larger bannertail kangaroo rats occasionally bounce from the ruts. They are as big as good-sized ground squirrels and, in order to balance their chunky bodies, have long black and white feathery streamers on the ends of their tails. Mostly, though, the road is used by the tiny desert cottontails, which nibble at its verges, and by scaled quail, taking their evening dust baths in the low places. The quail scoot back and forth in front of our wheels as erratically as circus wind-up toys, finally jumping into the air for short, stiff-winged glides into the Covillea creosote brush (*Larrea tridentata*). This dark green brush is sprinkled in spring with aromatic little yellow flowers and is good quail habitat. It blankets the western slopes of the Guadalupes and spreads out onto the plains until it is cut off to the west by the salt flats. Nothing grows between the widely spaced clumps, because toxins from the roots spread through the soil to inhibit the growth of grass or competing shrubs. It covers the prairie here only because of man, and cattle.

Creosote has always lived around the fringes of the Chihuahuan Desert, but only since the turn of the century has it spread across the plains and given much of West Texas, at least from a distance, the verdant look of rich pastureland. It is worthless as animal fodder, though. The fossilized scats of ground sloths from Aden Crater, New Mexico, contain bits of undigested creosote, and the Camp Verde camels ate the foliage when the army ran out of hay, but nothing else will touch it, including goats. Antelope, mule deer, and wild burros will starve rather than browse on the acrid leaves. Because of this, and its pervasive root toxin, the shrub now dominates the plains. For thousands of years though, before the cattle came, grass kept the creosote confined to the rocky canyons and scarps.

The grass was a climax vegetation of toboso and grama that stood densely, two feet high, like a fine-bristled hairbrush, and it covered the prairie and foothills below the peaks in the same shimmering waves that it spread across the great plains, up the center of the continent into northern Saskatchewan and Alberta. In Canada and the Midwest, the grass was a forest, growing six feet tall in the deep black soil that, after the bluestem and buffalo stands were plowed under, produced wheat fields. In the Trans-Pecos, the dirt was thin and pale with calcareous minerals, but because it has never been leached by much rainfall, it is richer than even the dark clay gumbos to the east, and the short grass that grew from it was a dozen times more nutritious than the coarser growth of the midwestern tall-grass prairies. It was also free, and for half

a century it spawned the dreams of cattlemen. For the most part, it brought them disaster, and they, in turn, brought ruin to the grasslands.

At the end of the Civil War, would-be ranchers drove enormous herds of Longhorns into the hundreds of empty square miles of Trans-Pecos pastures only to find that the rich grass lacked the protective backing of sod which cushioned the turf of eastern grazing grounds. Here, stones lay just beneath the thin topsoil, and the herds of up to five thousand animals—more concentrated than the wandering buffalo had ever been—rapidly pinched off the mat of roots between their hooves and the underlying rock. This, more than grazing, destroyed the grasslands. After the droughts of 1896 and 1905, the battered rootstock succumbed. Without grass cover, the topsoil was exposed to the constant gales off the scarps, which left only a desert pavement of limestone pebbles, covered with a new growth of creosote bushes by the 1920's.

Two of the first to see this pristine prairie as a potential cattle kingdom were Charles Goodnight and Oliver Loving. They made a fortune from cattle in West Texas just after the Civil War, but Goodnight went on to do his ranching in the Panhandle. In the Trans-Pecos, he and Loving were drovers. The end of the Confederacy had left Texas with an oversupply of Longhorns, hard to give away at four dollars a head, and cut off from the burgeoning eastern markets. Over the following fifteen years, Texans drove five million of them north to the railheads at Topeka, Abilene, and Dodge City—focal points of the ebullient new cattle culture which sprang up here during the seventies, based on the prospect of the open range. The availability of immense tracts of empty grassland free for the grazing was as exhilarating to the Victorian stockman as the acquisition of the horse had been to the foot-weary plains Comanche more than three hundred years before. Cattlemen could make quick fortunes pasturing seminomadic herds on the free range grass and then driving their stock hundreds of miles to take advantage of the large price disparities between markets. Cowhands worked for beans and bacon, plus ten dollars a month, and stockmen from all over the world poured onto the plains, drawn by opportunity. Charles Goodnight was one of them.

On June 6, 1866, Goodnight and Loving rode out of Belknap, Texas, behind a herd of two thousand Longhorns, headed for the booming New Mexico mining towns and high meat prices, where, even after losing weight on the trail, the steers would bring fifteen dollars each. Three weeks later, after pushing their cattle across sixty miles of waterless prairie beyond the Concho River, the drovers reached Fort Sumner on the Pecos, where the reservation Apaches were starving. The Goodnight-Loving Longhorns saved them, at the exorbitant price of eight cents a pound, paid by the Indian agent. Loving went on to Colorado with a small batch of breeding stock while Goodnight, with the profits, headed back to Central Texas for another herd. He almost failed to make it, since all his supply mules broke loose in a dust storm and, priorities being what they were, the first mule recovered was the one hauling the twelve thousand dollars in gold. The supply and water-hauling mules,

Sotol and maple leaves in Pine Spring Canyon.
Nikon FE. 28 mm Nikor lens.
Kodachrome.

meanwhile, were lost for good. It was a close shave for Goodnight, who would have died amid his bullion if it had not been for the last-minute appearance of a wagonload of watermelons, bound for the salt diggers of the Guadalupe flats. Bill Wilson joined Loving and Goodnight for another successful drive to New Mexico before winter, but the following year Loving's luck ran out. He and Wilson, racing competitors to the cattle buyers at Santa Fe, left Goodnight with their third herd, planning to cut across the northern Guadalupe range in a bid to reach the settlement early with news that the Longhorns were just behind, taking the long way around. They never made it to the mountains. Near the New Mexico border, some forty miles northeast of Pine Spring, they were intercepted by a Mescalero raiding party. In the shootout, Loving was too severely wounded to ride and hung on at the Pecos River for over a week while Wilson rode to Fort Sumner for help. Wilson and the cavalry made it back to Loving just in time and even got him to the fort, but he died there a few days later. Now, Loving, New Mexico, straggles along the wide banks of the Pecos—a ribbon creek in a river's bed this far north—near the site of the ambush.

Bill Wilson remained as a drover on what was by then known as the Goodnight-Loving Trail, and Goodnight started looking for a new partner willing to gamble for high stakes. He found John Chisum, an emphatic gentleman sporting an elongated, silver-plugged right earlobe. Jinglebob John and Goodnight attempted four more drives along the Pecos River route to Goodnight's holding pens at Bosque Grande, New Mexico; but Apache guerrillas had the drovers on the ropes by then, and their raids were too costly to sustain. After Chisum lost two successive herds of several thousand head to Mescalero, who swooped down out of the White Mountains one year and the Guadalupes the next, stampeding the steers into the desert where they could be butchered later, the pair finally split up. Ranching was the dream of every drover with a stake anyway, so Goodnight headed for North Texas while Chisum rode up into New Mexico. Within eight years, they had built the two largest cattle ranches ever established in the United States. In 1873, Chisum settled at South Spring, New Mexico, where, a year later, he was drawn into the Lincoln County range wars, along with notables like William Bonney and Pat Garrett. He emerged with over a million acres of land, stretching as far as Colorado and Kansas, harboring some eighty thousand (widely spaced) head of cattle. The *Las Vegas Gazette* for November 25, 1875, reported that Chisum's perimeter was "as far as a man can travel, on a good horse, in a summer."

Thirty years later, Robert Belcher saw the same plains west of the Guadalupe and Delaware ridges—whose thick grama grass had not been grazed since the drovers had pressed their herds through—and planned his own cattle kingdom. The only problem was water. Although the prairie was green for much of the year, there were no permanent springs or creeks in a thousand square miles of grassland. The bison had been able to follow the rains hundreds of miles across the prairie and Longhorns were good long-distance trotters, too. But by the turn of the

century, beef cattle meant heavy-bodied Herefords, and they needed waterholes within a couple of miles of their pastures. Belcher figured that,
if the windmill had allowed Herefords to prosper on the Panhandle's dry
stubble, permanent stock tanks in the tall grass of the Trans-Pecos
could support even larger herds. Ground water here was too deep—
2,300 feet—for windmill wells anyway, so Belcher went up to the flowing springs high along the mountain bluffs. Cattle could not make it up
the steep canyons to the lowest pools, but men could. Men carrying
water pipe.

With enormous labor, Belcher and his Mexican crew cantilevered
nearly two miles of pipe into an aquaduct snaking up through the boulders of Bone Canyon to the spring-fed pools that lie halfway to the scarp.
The pipe fed a stock tank in the foothills below, the only permanent
water for fifty miles across the prairie. Belcher commissioned architect
John Smith to build, overlooking the tank, a saltbox clapboard house
that looks as though it should sit on the coast of Maine. There was still
no real road through the Guadalupes in 1908, and Belcher took a week
to haul the milled siding by mule team from Van Horn. The house, and
the ranch, were for his new bride. She looked at the stark gray-gabled
dwelling—a dot on the treeless slopes three thousand feet below El
Capitan. The nearest companionship other than her husband was two
days' ride away over a rocky mule trail. The next morning, she took off
for the East. Belcher soon followed, leaving the place to his brother,
Henry, who stayed seven years with his wife and daughter before the
1915 drought drove them out as well. Now, gusts of wind pour across the
porch and tear through its carved columns, sounding like rollers of surf
in the dark.

Between the walking-stick chollas that fill Belcher's old front yard,
we unfurl our gear at sundown. Despite the regular first-night equipment *paseo* at the campgrounds, no paraphernaliaphile has yet braved
Michael's dour, grizzle-bearded mien to inquire about the mountain of
formidable machinery lashed beneath rip-stop nylon across the top of
his Kelty pack. They should have, for, despite the ironmonger's camera
box with its agriculturally sturdy sliding tracks and enormous wooden
tripod, Michael is one of them. His desk is a collapsed newsstand of
Wilderness Camping, Audubon and *Signal Smoke, Natural History,
Canoe and Canoeist, The Smithsonian, Outside,* and *Outdoor Life.* Between their layers, corners folded, marginalia scrawled everywhere,
their order sheets long missing, are the mother lodes: catalogues from
Eastern Mountain Sports, Early Winters and R.E.I. of Seattle, JanSport,
Class 5, Herter's of Mitchell, South Dakota, and L. L. Bean.

Allender comes to the Guadalupes only slightly less well prepared
than a member of the final assault team flung against a yet-unclimbed
Himalaya. His own careful stitchery holds together a pair of elaborate,
high-collared parkas he made for himself and his wife, Susan, in which
they resemble blue Michelin men carrying an extra tire around their
faces; but the masterwork in his technological armory is an equally
bulbous hand-sewn Gor-Tex sleeping bag (Eddie Bauer, $239.99). Hoyt

and I are careful to note how tight the seams are cinched and how well the down is distributed, which gives Allender such a kick that he hauls the bag, and nothing else, straight out into the blustery desert, wishing only that it were colder, although he won't have to bundle in with his Nikon and light meter to keep them from freezing solid, the way he must in the high country on top.

There is no protective flap above the bag's headrest, which offers an uninterrupted view of the stars, but which, after a handful of restless, windburned nights, gives Allender a puffy, boiled-crab visage that he cheerfully accepts as one of his mountain-man dues. Hoyt seems to have taken an equally strong draught of wilderness mystique during two days in the car with Michael en route from Roswell and, despite his single Navaho blanket, sandals, and thin denims, also elects to sleep out in the brush.

My gear is intermediate: mostly olive drab 1950's scout, with a smattering of slightly more recent aromatic army surplus. No one is very interested in it at the Pine Spring equipment parades, and I intend to use as little of it as possible. Hiding from the wind, I scrunch into the cab of my truck to sleep whenever I can. The gusts get stronger after

McKittrick Creek in upper South McKittrick Canyon.
Arca Swiss 4 × 5. 90 mm Schneider lens. Ektachrome.

Texas madrone tree.
Nikon FE. 55 mm micro Nikor lens. Kodachrome.

midnight, rocking the old Ford half-ton on its springs; but I hardly notice, even when Hoyt squeezes in on the floor. Before dawn, he's out again, fumbling with Allender's light meter and checking the eastern sky. An hour later, the pair are back, ravenous from an unsuccessful foray across the flats in hopes of framing a sufficiently distant perspective of the escarpment's long dawn shadows over the desert. Hoyt has brought no food, but Allender is never short of provisions and is so glad to have a real audience for his talents at the campfire—he has long since given up on me with my fruit and Granola—that he is inspired to break out his new Whole Earth Provision Company reflector oven and add the flourish of pancakes, bacon, and sourdough biscuits to his usual breakfast entrée of oatmeal and chocolate.

By six, the sky is solid blue, but the air is still cool: fifty-three degrees. As we start our climb up Bone Canyon, the rusted remnants of Belcher's pipeline lie about us, twisted by the floods that have torn it loose from its moorings on the canyon walls, twenty feet above the bed. The walls appear to have been built with millions of adobe bricks, uniformly two inches thick, stacked several hundred feet high. That is close to what they are. Jack Naumann, a geologist from Texas Tech who is studying the formation, showed me that the apparent bricks are multiple layers of mud shale—compacted detritus ground by waves off the oceanward face of the old barrier reef which now forms the rimrock, three quarters of a mile above us. Since these deposits were the first sediments worn off the reef, 220 million years ago, they were buried deepest and compressed most uniformly. Now, uplifted, they are the oldest exposed rocks in the park.

During the tectonic adjustments that raised the reef, the cracks that split deep into its limestone wall began in the compacted layers of limestone shale, and it is the uniformity of their mud-brick structure that gives the mouths of all the Guadalupe canyons—Bone and neighboring Shumard, Dog, Pine Spring, and even McKittrick—their unpromising prospect. From without, they seem to be little more than sterile arroyos, leading a few hundred yards into the foothills; but just beyond the brown adobe of their mouths, the apparent shallow gullies steepen and ascend between high, sharply narrowed limestone walls which, farther up near the springs, are softened with lichen and fern banks.

As we climb into this zone, the brushy nests of cactus wrens, which are everywhere in the cholla below (since they typically build a dozen or so roosting nooks in addition to the main homestead), thin out, and canyon wrens take their place. They are shyer than their lowland counterparts, but we hear them constantly, piping tiny waterfalls of trills down the musical tone scale. The gorge is so narrow here that, from its center, we can see every detail of both walls, latticed with crevices. A black rock squirrel peeps from one, ducks in, and checks us out again from his upstairs balcony. Another crevice holds too much interest for one of the wrens and, while Michael climbs up to see if it is a nest, Hoyt and I notice that the blue strip of sky framed above him is filled with darting bank swallows. Earlier, a big falcon, probably a prairie on this western front, had sailed past high against the cliffs, dragging its darting shadow diagonally across the gorge. The wren's nest is far back in a crevice and Michael decides not to stick his hand in to investigate, partially out of deference to the agitated hen but mainly because the overhanging ledges offer shade to black-tailed rattlers. A deep strike in this inaccessible country would be a horror.

"I got bit on the ass by a rattlesnake once," Hoyt offers cheerfully. "Want to see the scars?" He shows us anyway. "I used to carry a razor. Figured if any of our bunch ever got bit, I'd slice open the bite and suck out the venom, which was the recommended procedure at the time. Then I sat down to sketch without looking and got bit right through my canvas pants. That's one way to find out who your real friends are."

As the climb steepens, we clamber over boulders the size of trucks, then houses, lodged between the waisted walls. It is sweaty going, and Hoyt is both frail and over seventy. But he is looking for gold. The night before, he read and was taken by a Park Service plaque which begins: "Stories of hidden gold go back to Spanish days. The conquistadores who rode north from Mexico wrote about fabulous deposits." Geronimo—the notorious one—liked to watch the white-eyes spend their energies fruitlessly scouring the Guadalupe canyons in search of a mother lode, and he elaborated on the conquistador legend during his long stay in army detention camps in Florida and Oklahoma. Prospector Ben Sublett apparently did carry out some nuggets around 1875, reportedly scooped up in handsful from the floors of three small caves that pock the face of McKittrick Canyon's north wall just inside its entrance. Sublett may also have carried the nuggets in, however, perhaps hoping to capitalize on a subsequent land rush, for no others have been found anywhere in the Guadalupes. That doesn't deter Hoyt, though, and he scrambles along like an emphysemic mountain goat, fueled by the possibility of an odd nugget. In his wake, I slip and lurch, cursing the loose footing. Michael struggles with the spiky magnitude of his format camera, swearing his mild "dagnab it!" profanity: Bogart and Tim Holt in *Treasure of the Sierra Madre*, grimily sweating up the Mexican Rockies behind little white-haired Walter Huston, springing from rock to rock in the lead.

Then Hoyt pulls up, hit with vertigo and unable to breathe. Visions of CPR float before me, and Michael begins to mentally gird himself for the carry-out. "If anything should happen to me . . . ," Paul stammers, wide-eyed and panting, with an upward glance at the ever-present vultures. He gulps. "Just send that sweet little Caroline Wilson . . . with a sleeping bag!" It is his joke of the day, and we get it the rest of the way up the canyon, spliced into a running account of his struggles over the rocks. Hoyt's wobbly balancing act doesn't interfere with his verbal coordination, and listening to him is like listening to Cosell at ringside. Except that Hoyt is his own Ali.

Before he cut silhouettes, Hoyt was an ice sculptor. He started in Boston, carving swans at weddings and banquets, moved up to Christmas nativity scenes and, finally, to memorial-sized outdoor statues of

Roots of a dead cottonwood tree in
Bone Canyon.
Arca Swiss 4 × 5. 90 mm Schneider lens.
Ektachrome.

Apache plume in flower and seed in
Bone Canyon.
Arca Swiss 4 × 5. 210 mm Schneider lens.
Ektachrome.

ice on frozen ponds that would last all winter in New England. Then the American Geographical Society heard of Hoyt and decided it would be a fine idea to have their most famous alumnus, Admiral Peary, memorialized by a truly enormous ice statue. The sculpture was to include both Peary and the commodore's former valet and right-hand man, carved from the ice flow floating directly over the North Pole, where, according to plan, it would remain a perpetual, or at least long-lasting, frozen monument to the explorer. No helicopter could make it that far north in those postwar days, so Hoyt was to parachute over the pole in early June, set up camp alone, carve his monolith, and then be picked up by a ski-plane, if one could get in, at the height of summer a few weeks later.

Hoyt chickened out, and the monument went unbuilt. He gave up ice sculpture for photography and eventually went to work for Polaroid, developing packs to adapt instant film to the large-format cameras. Years later, he was demonstrating the latest of Edwin Land's technology to a group of luminaries in New York when one of the city's smaller blackouts occurred. While Hoyt was in the basement trying in vain to turn the power back on, one of the luminaries, who had had a lot of practical experience, offered to help.

"Name's Byrd."

"Not Admiral Byrd?" Hoyt was thunderstruck. "Have I got a story for you!"

Admiral Byrd was equally thunderstruck at the possibility of being upstaged and decided he needed his own icy Rushmore on an appropriate Antarctic bluff, as large as Paul could carve it. The explorer approached his backers with the idea of the sculptor accompanying his next expedition, but the financiers thought it a vain and whimsical notion on Byrd's part and quashed the idea. Hoyt still has the bug, though, and confidentially tells me how he has eyed pink cliffs above us with visions of a jackhammer crew under his direction chiseling out a gargantuan frieze of neolithic men, Apaches, and prospectors; but he knows better than to even mention such things to Michael.

At Bone Spring, there are big cottonwoods—the only place they grow in the park. They are also the only trees on the western escarpment, and they shade the pools and lushly flutter their leaves against the stark cliffs above. The night before, from the porch of Belcher's house, we saw mourning doves flying into the mouth of the canyon and knew that meant there was water in the spring. The insectivorous wrens, orioles, and ash-throated flycatchers can subsist in the desert solely on the moisture from their prey, but mourning doves eat only dry seeds and must, therefore, seek out ponds to drink, morning and evening. Bone Spring is the only water for many miles along the western side of the mountains, and its smooth pools, cloistered with cottonwoods, are a dovecote. As we lie prone to scoop water from them, the doves flutter in soft gray flocks about us, tame as pigeons in a loft, cooing and bumping each other aside for drinking space.

There is more canyon to climb, even rougher above the spring, and then the long descent into the falling western sun. Michael and I are

midway down a long, flaky rubble of boulders with a dropoff at its lower
lip when a clatter of pebbles passes us from behind.

"Stop, damn it! That's an order!" Michael barks back up the slope
at Hoyt, flinging himself across the loose shale to the left, getting between Hoyt and the dropoff. He had seen Hoyt's legs begin to buckle
and, mother-henning, leapt to take the shock of his fall. After awhile,
however, Hoyt makes it on his own and then, just as gamely, slowly
shins over the rest of the drops, right on down to Williams Ranch. He is
impressed by the canyon and the rimrock beyond but not intimidated,
in spite of the fact that he looks as though he could use a couple of
scouts just to cross the porch.

Two ridges over from Bone Canyon, the big Guadalupe rift empties
westward into the pass itself. Four miles beyond its mouth, Pine Spring
Café is still the only building along U.S. 180 between Signal Peak trailer
camp on the western side of the mountains and park headquarters in
the eastern foothills. It is owned and run by Bertha Glover. One snowy
morning I retrieved her venerable chihuahua, Pancho, who was wearing
a red-and-white knitted sweater, from the wrong side of the highway,
and she told me how she had come here as a bride, in 1917. The only
Anglo neighbor her side of El Paso was Dolph Williams, who had just
taken over the Belcher Ranch. Although most of the grass was gone by
then, Williams and his Indian companion, Geronimo—a name as common among the Mescalero as Smith or Ford among Anglos—were
making a go of it feeding two thousand sheep on the remaining rootstock, sometimes sheltering them on top of the fossil bones in the cave
that still bears his name. Williams ran the ranch until his death in 1942,
but he was a bachelor and was lonesome there, too. Back in the twenties, he used to ride over Guadalupe Pass a lot to visit the Glovers,
following a trail that only he could pick out through the network of
canyons. Bertha Glover is sorry that neither of the Belcher wives stayed
but doesn't believe it is, or ever was, a man's country. She told me she
had already outlasted her husband, Williams, and most of the other old-
timers by a good many years and intended to outlast them by a good
many more. The sign on her door reads: MEN MUST WEAR SHIRTS NO
DOGS ALLOWED.

Just over a mile up Guadalupe Canyon from the highway cut
stands an enormous alligator juniper. Its bid to live here, far below the
boreal uplands, is all but extinguished—another victim of the drought,
still in progress. Only a few of the topmost branches remain green, but
the mass of the trunk suggests the foliage that the tree once spread here.
I wrap myself around it, arms extended, above the bulging root bolls.
Chest high, it takes three of my spans to circle the trunk. Tucked
behind the serpentine roots—which are virtual anacondas—in what
would have once been the only shade between El Capitan and the salt
flats, are the rubbled walls of two rooms, each no more than seven feet
on a side. Dug into the mountainside, the ruins overlook the lip of
Guadalupe Canyon as it spills away to the west, two thousand feet

above the desert floor. The dugout could have been built a quarter-mile higher in the canyon, close to a pair of flowing springs and shaded by a stand of dwarfed chinkapin oaks, but that would have meant giving up the view, and Geronimo Segura was not willing to do that. There is no historical litter among the stones, and the ruins suggest an archaeological dig, although they were the home of Williams' partner during the whole first half of the twentieth century. Geronimo married a Mexican lady, assumed her last name, and, with her, scraped out this little stone platform high on the eastern wall of Guadalupe Canyon, where, in the shelter of the big juniper, they raised seven daughters. Four of them, Sarah, Lupe, Rosa, and Lilly, worked for Bertha Glover, first on the ranch, and then at Pine Spring Café. One by one, the daughters moved to California, and Bertha now sees them only every few years when they visit Señora Segura, who lives just up the road in Carlsbad.

Between lecture tours for Polaroid, Hoyt traveled as a professional photographer, and, here, without a camera, he feels redundant—a useless old-timer, aesthetically out to pasture. For a couple of days, he carries Michael's lenses, offering optical advice like a golf caddy. In his photography, Michael is the ultimate loner—I am lucky to be shown a handful of transparencies, culled from hundreds, every six months—but now he consults Hoyt every time he unscrews a lenscap. "Think we'll be able to stop it down enough under that cloud? What about the magenta in those shadows?" Mutual technical know-how is not enough, however. The next morning, I watch Hoyt slide down a treacherous arroyo bank with Michael's Nikon clutched in one hand, its neckstrap flapping below. I was there, a month before, when Allender unpacked the instrument, a new FE model, gently laying out the lenses on a folded towel, wiping each one with silicone optical cloth; but he handed the camera over to Hoyt in a second. As Paul roller-derbies toward us in the bottom of the ravine, Michael is mild and pleasant. "How about putting that strap over your head?" he suggests. But he says it through gritted teeth.

Hoyt is oblivious, caught up in the rejuvenation of "burning film" again, snapping away at anything with a shadow or a speck of color, although he does flip the band around his neck. It doesn't do much good, since the eighty- to two-hundred-millimeter Nikkor lens sticks out a foot beyond his elbow, careening fore and aft as he flails through the boulders. All day, I watch that lens, unheeded by Hoyt, pick a random, lurching path through minefields of jagged limestone outcroppings. Michael sees it too, but in his view he has done all he can by asking Paul to be careful. It is obvious that prudence is the last thing in Hoyt's mind, but somehow, every time the camera's pendulum trajectory sweeps it toward a doom of splintering glass, Hoyt automatically hitches his shoulder and an inch of air appears beneath the lens at the ultimate instant, floating it smoothly between Scylla and Charybdis. By the second evening, Hoyt is replete, having burned eleven rolls of film past the long lens. The Nikon is only slightly scathed, and Michael happily folds it back into its green felt case.

Turtle Rock above McKittrick Creek.
Arca Swiss 4 × 5. 210 mm Schneider lens.
Ektachrome.

Two weeks later, we get a long, rambling letter from Hoyt. He is a changed man, he reports: our trip to the mountains was the catalyst. It seems to have burst an adolescent tide in Hoyt, who is nothing if not impulsive. He has gone back to Truth or Consequences, but only temporarily, to formally split up with Lois and his eight-year-old son before lighting out on his own like Huck, for the territory, ahead of the rest. The territory is indefinite—an archaeologist friend from the University of New Mexico has encouraged him to join their summer dig, for one thing, but it will be photographed: Hoyt has resurrected his cameras from nineteen years of storage. Michael is not surprised. He saw that Paul was in a bad way at Roswell, in need of affirmation, and offered him both a temporary hideout with us and a more or less genuine purpose for being there. The Nikon took its lumps for a reason.

Ponderosa pine, velvet ash, and Texas madrone trees near Pine Spring campground.
Arca Swiss 4 × 5. 210 mm Schneider lens. Ektachrome.

Limestone cliffs and blue sky reflected in
North McKittrick Creek behind a small composite.
Nikon FE. 55 mm micro Nikor lens. Kodachrome

Michael Allender
© '80

7

September 30, 1965

Saw two coyotes chasing nine deer (yearlings and two fawns). The deer ran as a group—one coyote on top of ridge—other one halfway down. Deer came to a halt and two does gave chase to the coyotes. 6:30 A.M.

January 21, 1966

Had a six-inch snowstorm today—moved ¼ mile southwest of Ranger Station—saw one coyote stalking a deer on the side of a draw; process went on for ten minutes. Finally, three large does came up behind the coyotes and ran him off. 4 P.M.

—GUADALUPE MOUNTAINS NATIONAL PARK
WILDLIFE FILE: MAMMALS

G UADALUPE MOUNTAINS NATIONAL PARK is one of the few places where you can see more wildlife by walking than you can sitting in a blind. Human pressure on animal populations is so great in most places that only the shy ones live to propagate, and they are seldom seen by hikers. Within the park, however, it is not unusual to hike right up to such ordinarily wary creatures as sharp-shinned hawks and gray foxes. This is the ideal environment for Allender's temperament, since he is on the move almost constantly, covering enormous stretches of ground like a ranging coyote. His eye for static images works best just short of a dead run.

The animals we notice at this pace are the prominent ones: elk and mule deer, soaring buteos, noisy Steller's jays, and glossy, pink-and-black Lewis' woodpeckers—lifelist rarities be damned. Smaller creatures usually take too much time; but the ladybugs are hard to miss, in spite of their size. This year, they have massed early, in May, for their annual warm-weather rendezvous. It is bigger than Willie Nelson's Fourth of July picnic. When ladybugs swarm in the peaks, they don't clump up in little clusters like they do in suburban gardens. There are too many of them here, and by the billions they spread over every tree, bush, and blade of grass for miles. Wing-shell to wing-shell, they form an undulating beadwork of orange-and-black enamel dots that look too shiny to be real: Made in Taiwan. Because they are actually predatory beetles, the vegetation benefits from the ladybugs, who scour it clean of

Coyote (*Canis latrans*) and blacktail jackrabbit (*Lepus californicus*)

aphids and sap-boring insect larvae. Whatever they are eating this time has already been devoured, since the underside of every leaf around Smith Spring is bare of other insects.

Late in the day, as we return from Smith Spring—one of the eastern palisade springs, deep in a maple grotto with Japanese-garden pools—Michael is ahead as usual, kicking aside the larger stones. It slows him down and allows me to keep up.

"Rattler!" he calls gleefully, and I jump with anticipation. One of my reasons for being here is to look for *Crotalus lepidus lepidus*, the endangered and beautifully mottled white or pink rock rattlesnake, for Joe Laszlo, curator of reptiles at San Antonio's Brackenridge Park Zoo. The first *lepidus* I saw alive only stayed that way a moment. I spotted him edging across a parking lot in the Davis Mountains just before a guest from Indian Lodge proudly dropped a suitcase on him, leaving the rattler as flat as Coyote after Roadrunner has lured him into the path of an oncoming semi. In his breeding room at the zoo, under banks of multiple-spectrum lights, with seasonally adjusted temperature and humidity controls as elaborately contrived as those in an archival vault, Laszlo can breed at least small populations of vanishing reptiles back into existence. I am looking for *lepidus* brood stock. Two other snakes are also on my wanted list: the *klauberi* subspecies of the rock rattler, which may or may not occur as far east as the Guadalupes, and the Trans-Pecos copperhead, *Agkistrodon contortrix laticinctus*. Like so many other animals, it is an anachronism in West Texas. Copperheads are woodland creatures everywhere in their range, with wide brown dorsal bands evolved for camouflage against the dappled shade of leafy forest floors. The widespread pluvial lowland woods in which the Trans-Pecos species used to live have now been narrowed by the spreading plains into vestigial stands of cottonwoods and elms around the few remaining permanent springs and creeks, and the snakes are concentrated there. In spite of this, Trans-Pecos copperheads are seldom seen, because they are rare, nocturnal, and very good at hiding in rocks and debris. The relic population living around these desert springs is able to make do in such a restricted habitat only because vipers as a group are sedentary reptiles that do not burn up much energy hunting for prey, and copperheads are among the most lethargic vipers. They afford their lethargy only by being extremely efficient hunters. Heat-sensing pits just behind the nostrils give them an effective, infrared radar scan, while their hypodermic venom delivery ensures that a bitten mouse will only make a couple of jumps. A single eight-inch jab is ordinarily the only movement required to get a meal. This low-energy ambush predation only works where a regular supply of small mammals can be counted on, but the water holes draw rodents every night. The vipers' approach still puts fewer mice in their bellies than fast-moving, open-country foragers like coachwhips are able to catch, but copperheads are compact animals, whose hard-times metabolism allows them to live atop a smaller biomass of prey animals than more active snakes of the same weight. At night, or in cool, rainy weather, they sometimes risk forays a mile or so out onto the plains—where their yellow-and-rust bands stand out against the leafless stubble—but they never leave the leafy shade around their springs when the desert sun might push their temperature to a fatal level in minutes.

Seven other serpents, all nonvenomous, also live only in the rocky desert and mountains west of the Pecos Canyon. Trans-Pecos rat snakes (*Elaphe subocularis*), gentle, delicate animals without a trace of the nasty disposition characteristic of their Central Texas relatives; rear-fanged lyre snakes (*Trimorphodon biscutatus*) with catlike eyes; beautiful beige and fawn Big Bend and mountain patch-nosed snakes (*Salvadora deserticola* and *S. grahamiae*), as well as an exotic group of kingsnakes, make this country as much a gathering place for herpetologists as it is for geologists and birders.

Most of the herpetologists' attention is focused on the gray-banded kings (*Lampropeltis mexicana alterna*). These shy creatures are colored like Oriental porcelains, with glossy gray or charcoal ground colors banded in black-edged vermilion brocade. There are at least four primary color phases, distinguished by shading as subtly altered as that of rugs from neighboring villages in Afghanistan. Each phase was once thought to live only in a few rocky canyons whose conditions fostered one color pattern over the others; but all of the phases have recently been found distributed so widely over the entire Chihuahuan Desert that the one-canyon, one-color adaptation theory is in eclipse. The kingsnakes' habitat drew so much interest primarily because the reptiles are valuable—exceptionally vivid specimens bring hundreds of dollars on the snake black market from reptile buffs all over the world, and the location of the best canyons was closely guarded information among collectors. Because of their value, and because they were so easily caught along roads at night, the small population of gray-banded kings in Texas came under such pressure from collectors that, in 1977, the species was awarded the slim protection of endangered status. Game wardens now cruise the ranch roads during the peak hunting period in late May, stopping the multibeamed pickups used for nighttime spotlighting to check the screen topped plastic canisters, covered with moistened burlap, which everyone uses to hold the catch.

The little lizard-eating *lepidus* rattlers (as well as the Trans-Pecos copperhead, and Baird's and Trans-Pecos rat snakes) were also designated as endangered at the same time, but the rattlers' protection is only from collectors who pick them up on the roads or (rarely) extricate them from the broken rock fields where they live. It is still legal to kill any rattlesnake that poses a threat to one's safety, and *lepidus* rattlers may be legally killed by anyone at any time, just not caught for trade or resale. Except for the herpers—as snake buffs call each other—a rattler in West Texas is still vermin, though, and if it's not extinct, it's not rare enough for most people. The Indian Lodge guest was in no danger of standing before a judge. Rock rattlers never threaten anyone, however, because they are so wary, alert, and agile that they drop into the myriad crevices lacing their rock-terraced homes at the first vibration set off by a man crunching up the hill, and the only people ever bitten by them are herpetologists and reptile fanciers handling captive specimens. When this happens, though, it is likely to be serious: J. P. Jones, herpetology curator at the Fort Worth Zoo, was in intensive care for six days during the fall of 1979 following the bite of an eighteen-inch *lepidus*. Like many snakes that feed on cold-blooded prey, these little rattlers have very potent venom, with more neurotoxic components than that of mammal-feeding serpents—whose evolution has given them quicker-acting hemorrhagic venoms designed to drop fleeing rodents in their tracks. Although hematoxins cause great pain and tissue necrosis, the damage is likely to be localized in animals as large as human beings, posing less threat to life than the more generalized venoms of many of the reptile-feeding snakes.

Most captive rock rattlesnakes were originally picked up, like the gray-banded kings, on unpaved ranch tracks at night, where they behave quite differently than they do in the daytime rock fields. As ambush hunters, all the pit vipers have lost the open-ground speed of the non-venomous snakes, and, quick as *lepidus* are within the narrow confines of their limestone homes, they are still too slow to make a break for it across even the limited flat ground of a gravel roadbed. Instead, they lie quite still when spotlighted, hiding in the camouflage of a milky coloration, which in this part of the Trans-Pecos almost exactly matches the chalky, decayed limestone of the Guadalupe range. Eighty miles to the south, the Davis Mountain population is the same rusty pink as that region's volcanic granite boulders, while in the slightly moister climate of both the western Edwards Plateau and the high valleys of the Mexican sierras, where lichen encrusts the crumbly stones, rock rattlers have a greenish cast. They are primarily nocturnal everywhere, but even in moonlight their pale coloration would stand out were it not for the jagged black bands and splotches that cross their bodies every few inches, breaking up the animals' outline by approximating the network of dark cracks lacing the shattered limestone of the desert floor. Trans-Pecos rat snakes and gray-banded kingsnakes also have dark crossbands that match their crevice-filled backgrounds, but, since their lowland habitat is too hot for daytime foraging, they are even more exclusively nocturnal than the rock rattlers—and are more intensely colored. Like deep-sea corals and fishes whose vivid primary hues are never seen except with artificial light, these reptiles have also evolved brilliant patterns of red and mustard which appear only as shades of gray in the limited, short-wave-length spectrum visible by moonlight. Even on the roads, they are almost impossible to see in automobile headlights, looking like small charcoal sticks until they are hit with the direct beam of an incandescent spot.

The theory behind road collecting, of course, is that the still-warm pavement draws the herps out for a bit more radiant energy before the chill of night slows their ectothermic metabolisms down. There are big, flat sun-warmed rocks scattered everywhere across the desert that retain more warmth than asphalt but which do not attract serpents after dark; and several species are seen on the roads only between midnight and dawn, long after the pavement has chilled. Most snakes, in fact, are just crossing the roads in their nocturnal forays when they are unlucky enough to fall into someone's headlights, although some species seem to like the smooth, open pavement regardless of its temperature and lie patiently on it, waiting to be investigated by the mice which are common in the roadside grass. Since there is often a long wait between herps in driving the back roads all night at twenty miles per hour, herpers have a tendency to develop beer bellies and look for snakes in convivial groups. The only road through the Guadalupes is the interstate highway, though, and, since no reptile in its right mind would crawl out on it, snake searches here are conducted on foot. The pace is too slow for Allender, but it suits me fine.

The rattler in front of us is not one of the rarer species, unfortunately. It is a common western diamondback, an *atrox*, and a small one at that. Even a five-footer would make our day, and this little fellow is only half that size, but Michael is too much of a herper to let even this minimal opportunity go by. He already has the closeup lens on his Nikon as he flops down beside the snake. It folds into coils, rearing and buzzing like a small vibrator as I scoot it around with a stick, trying to set it up for the camera. Michael clicks away. There are other hikers on their way up the trail, though, and to avoid a confrontation I carry the rattler off to a juniper stand and release it, still whirring with rage.

A popular poster among reptile buffs reads, "Stop Rattlesnake Roundup Slaughter," over a picture of a coiled diamondback. It never cut any ice with me. My ecological sympathies just didn't stretch that far. Until I started hanging around with herpers. (Like birders, herpers know each other, in person and by reputation. The directors of the Houston Zoo, the Fort Worth Nature Center, Austin's Natural Science Center, and the Armand Bayou Nature Center are all herpers. Guadalupe Mountains National Park's resident herper is Jim Grace, who is from Texas Tech. Nothing lights up the day for any of them like finding a rare snake, and nothing makes them madder than the automatic killing of creatures which are no less valid inhabitants of the planet than human beings.) Now the possibility of a rarity beneath the next rock has evaporated most of my old fear and loathing. I am searching for reptilian pieces of eight. A fallen yucca trunk lying just off the path offers enough shade to preserve a little more moisture than the surrounding flats, and prickly pear have taken advantage of the marginally preferable habitat and grown up around it. Allender pokes beneath the shaggy cactus log with a stick. It looks like a perfect spot for a big mojave rattler, and, when he lets out a whoop, I join him two feet in the air. He is headed over the log, though, grabbing with both hands at a long, brown streak whipping back and forth like a runaway balloon. As Michael scoops it up, the snake twists backward and bites him rapidly several times, leaving small razorlike scratches across his forearm. This is par for the course in herp collecting, though, and Allender hardly notices, waving the snake over his head at me in the joy of capture. "I don't know what he is, but he was moving too fast to be a bad one."

He is a desert striped whipsnake, five feet long but no thicker than my thumb. Horizontal brown and white stripes run backward from a tiny head as pointed as if it had been through a pencil sharpener, with bulging dark eyes that stare along furrows recessed into each side of its snout. This adaptation allows the animal to see directly ahead, where its overlapping right and left visual fields provide a narrow, three-dimensional band. Enhanced depth perception is vital to its predatory style, for whipsnakes are fast, diurnal-pursuit serpents that slither down the darting prairie racerunner and whiptail lizards of the desert floor. Released, this one streaks away through the brush, but before it has gone twenty yards it forgets its close shave with us and freezes, head a foot from the ground, studying a little oblong mound where one of the whiptails is hidden under a layer of soil. We wait a quarter-hour before flushing the lizard, which streaks off with a tiny explosion of sand. Spooked again, the whipsnake forgets its hunger and flows back into its original prickly pear patch in the lee of the yucca.

The popular fascination with serpentine phalluses has also come to seem absurd to me: a bizarre preoccupation of people unfamiliar with the subject. There is just no room for that sort of thing in this harsh country, where every animal struggles to endure the fierce climate, hide from man and predators, and eat whatever it can catch in between. As has always been the case, some species are making a better go of it than others, and nobody is more sympathetic to how hard it is for even the successful ones to survive than Allender. And he is a herper from way back.

As a teenager, Michael lived for awhile in a cave dug into the wall of a canyon as far from his parents' home in Dalhart as he could hike in a day. One of his preoccupations was catching prairie rattlers by digging them out of their dens. "The standard thing that kids do," he remembers. "Because they were dangerous, and because they had a rattle, they were a lot neater than plain old slick-tailed snakes." The big ones became belts; the smaller ones, hatbands. But that was before Michael had his herpetological consciousness raised. I think it reached its zenith in 1967, when Michael was sent to Big Bend to monitor pesticide residues for Texas A&M. With pride, he wrote me about winning his herper's stripes:

> Midway through the summer my study area was shifted to the Chisos Mountains—a cool relief. I was camped near a switchback on the winding road leading up to Green Gulch from the Basin. I chatted with a ranger collecting bats in nets nearby, and then turned in. I was awakened when a car stopped on the road, so I climbed out of my sleeping bag and made my way through the brush to the edge of the road and crouched there . . . in my underwear. Illuminated by the lights of the car, I could see a black-tailed rattlesnake. The

driver retreated to the trunk of his car and came back holding a shovel. That was too much for me. Surprise was definitely on my side as I rushed out and grabbed the snake by the tail—no time for fancy neck-pinning maneuvers. I had to twirl it over my head to keep its body stretched out and the fangs away from me, but I caught a brief look at the man's face as I ran by. It held the most startled, unbelieving expression I have ever seen.

Alligator juniper tree in Pine Spring Canyon.
Nikon FE. 28 mm Nikor lens.
Kodachrome.

Michael Allender
© '80

8

June 19, 1973

Bobcat—Dog Canyon Ranger Station—full of porcupine quills. Died about 3:30 P.M.

—GUADALUPE MOUNTAINS NATIONAL PARK
WILDLIFE FILE: MAMMALS

FOURTEEN MILES LONG, not counting Capitan bluff, and sometimes three-quarters of a mile high, the eastern Guadalupe palisade is a solid slab of scored limestone rising out of the desert foothills, but it is only a façade. The real cordillera begins a half-mile behind this facing. For twenty miles between the narrow outer wall and the main range runs the deepest and most spectacular of the Guadalupe canyons, so effectively protected from the meteorological vicissitudes of the Chihuahuan Desert by the wall of this escarpment that its upper reaches are as heavily forested as a wooded fjord. The flanking rocky bluffs are damp with cracks leading in from mountain aquifers, and ferns grow along the seeps.

Some two miles beyond its desert mouth, Harry and Sharla Lord live, in Wallace Pratt's old stone house, near the junction where McKittrick Canyon forks into its long north and south tributaries. A road used to snake up the clear creek which furrows the canyon's floor, but it has been closed for years, and only a rocky trail remains. Harry and Sharla hike in and out every day, hauling food, firewood, and laundry, after Harry has finished his eight-hour patrol up the ridges and into the high country. A drilled well provides them plenty of water. Their house is beautiful and spare, almost empty of furniture. In a corner is Sharla's music stand; her instruments lie in cases on the floor. She is the infection control officer at Guadalupe Medical Center in Carlsbad, which means getting up at five for the two-mile hike and fifty-mile drive to the hospital. She also teaches microbiology three times a week. "I was going to give my students a research project until I went to the library in town and found it wouldn't have done them much good." She shrugs, smiling. Harry is also an intellectual, with a slight hesitation in his speech that gives his deliberate sentences a suggestion of seminar classrooms. He has been a park ranger here for five years and, despite his thinning hair, still appears to be the same gangly Boy Scout he was seventeen years

Bobcat (*Lynx rufus*) and Steller's jay
(*Cyanocitta stelleri*)

ago. He thinks he could live in these mountains for the rest of his life, although he knows that would be asking too much of Sharla.

Pratt Lodge is a Hansel and Gretel house, squeezed between dark pillars of alligator juniper and built totally of stone: walls, roof, and floor. The stones are big slabs of dense, finely grained aphanitic lime-stone standing together edge to edge. The gaps are laced with smaller plates of all colors. Shape was the only thing that counted with the masons, and adjacent slabs are pink, chocolate, tan, white, and gray, as long as they fit. The result is a marvelous calico structure standing alone far up in the gorge, where, even in June, the high bluffs stall sunrise and cut off the afternoon glare into dusk after four. It is cool inside, and I feel slightly intrusive, like a spelunker in the big empty living room. No stalagtites; the beams that support the unlined flagstone roof are joined with dowels. Harry twists one dowel free and goes out back. He has to bend far over to open the door because Harry is tall and all the door latches, and the light switches as well, are just above knee height. Pratt was an old bachelor when he had the house built in 1926 by an even older German stonemason and three Mexican apprentices. He must have also been a leprechaun. Down in the woods, the dowel from Harry's living room fits exactly into a curving line of holes bored into a dead tree. By the time the tree died, sometime in the forties, a good deal of bark had grown over the line of bored holes, but enough remain to spell JUAN S.

The largest of the slate tablets, laid flat, stretches three feet by ten beneath the alligator juniper leaning over the kitchen door. It is the Lords' summer dining table. In December, orange maple leaves are scat-tered across its dark top, and because winter is a lonely time up in the canyon, I am a welcome visitor. Sharla has coffee, and we all sit on the sunny end of the table with our cups. Around us live elk, cougars, a great many mule deer, and an occasional bear. The bears leave piles of their droppings, or scat, under favorite scat trees, the nearest of which grows at the mouth of McKittrick's middle fork, a quarter mile from Harry and Sharla's back door. Everyone who sees a bear reports it:

September 9, 1977
I sighted the bear along the McKittrick Ridge trail. . . . It was lying down. It saw me first. It ran north over a ridge. I had been within 50 yards of the bear and observed it for thirty seconds before it went out of sight. Cinnamon color, darker towards legs. 27–30 inches at shoulder. Weight—approximately 285–325 lbs. 6:05 P.M. Partly cloudy. 70°, light wind.

—HARRY STEED, USNPS
GUADALUPE MOUNTAINS NATIONAL PARK
WILDLIFE FILE: MAMMALS

The only other bears in Texas live seven hundred miles away in the Big Thicket. They are remnants of the old eastern woodland popula-tion and are almost never seen because of the dense cover they inhabit.

A sotol perched on a boulder above a group of *Senecio* in South McKittrick Canyon.
Arca Swiss 4 × 5. 210 mm Schneider lens. Ektachrome.

In the wide open terrain of West Texas, black bears occur in a number of places, from the Bofecillos Mountains to the Devil's River Canyon along the Mexican border, with a few ranging north as far as the Davis Mountains and the southern Edwards Plateau. Guadalupe Park's bears are a different, remnant population of Rocky Mountain animals living on the long montane ridges stretching tenuously down across the desert from Colorado to the Mexican Sierras. Until the 1880's, the high country had such a dense population of bears that soldiers from Fort Bliss in El Paso were given hunting leave to practice their aim on safaris to the Guadalupe uplands. Only a few of the bears survived, and for nearly a hundred years they remained, very fearful of man, in the remotest parts of the high country. With the closing of the goat ranches and outlawed trapping, the bears are increasing again, their numbers reinforced with adolescent cubs—shoulders dyed red for at least a year's identification—trapped and moved south from the Lincoln National Forest. There are still fewer bears than the range can support, but in the last few years they have gotten braver about extending their territory and have even begun to venture into McKittrick Canyon again, down to their old scat tree.

There are also fifty-five mule deer to the square mile in McKittrick, which means the narrow canyons are home to more than a hundred deer. In bad weather, they bunch up below Pratt Lodge under the stands of juniper and piñon pine along McKittrick Creek. They are easy prey then, and snowstorms draw cougars down from the rimrock on the trail that runs past the Lords' porch.

In clear weather, mountain lions work hard for a kill. Like eagles, they are unable to live on the limited prey they can take from even a rich habitat like McKittrick Canyon and, therefore, have to roam widely to find enough to eat. In this terrain, the home range of a single cat can encompass 100,000 acres—an area greater than the entire park—but, since their boundaries are their own, at any given time the park may constitute a portion of the territories of half a dozen cougars. Unfortunately, that leaves each individual vulnerable to trapping over the majority of its range, particularly since most of it covers adjacent sheep and goat ranches whose free-ranging livestock is easy, almost natural, prey for the big cats. Four years ago, after two nearby ranches had lost thirty sheep by midsummer, the National Park Service laid plans for predator control specialist Roy McBride to hunt the Coyote Peak area with dogs and a tranquilizer dart gun, in hopes of relocating the errant cats in South Texas. No cougars were caught, though, and when the nearby Hughes Ranch lost sixty sheep in the first few months of 1978, the ranchers didn't wait around again. On July 23, the cat—a 150 pound male—was trapped and shot on the west rim just north of the park in Otero County, New Mexico.

On summer afternoons, the most prominent wildlife along the trail which follows McKittrick Creek up the canyon are orange-and-black burrowing bees. In every shady spot where the earth is soft enough, the air is cut with swarms of them ferrying to and from their burrows. They do not sting, so it is safe to stand in the middle of one of their buzzing gyres, watching one bee after another break formation and peel off straight at the ground. Always on target, they plummet right down the smokestacks: holes the size of pencils, puncturing the soil. Below is another kind of apian community—a nuclear family, single dwelling burrow organization quite different from the communal honeybee hive. In the evenings, the bees are all in their burrows, and above them hognosed skunks snuffle along the trail. They root like bears with their long foreclaws, digging out the individual stores of honey and larval bees, especially during the last two weeks in June, when both honey and grubs are in greatest supply.

Living in the canyon sometimes means wading alone up the creek after dark, or in bad weather, but most of the time the two-mile hike home is an idyll for the Lords. Sharla saw a badger on the trail just after sunup in June, "carrying a good-size snake in its mouth; I couldn't tell what kind," and Harry had an even better sighting: after checking its tracks for weeks, he glimpsed a little spotted cougar near the turnstile entry gate to the canyon. Five months later, Harry and Sharla are still as excited over them as they are about the year-old lion tracks by their porch steps. Neither is a trained naturalist, and Harry has only recently identified all the trees around Pratt Lodge, but even when they are unable to name most of its plants, birds, and insects, they are exhilarated just by living in the wild canyon every day.

It is an expensive privilege. The Park Service frowns on rangers' wives working for the same administration, and Sharla's job in Carlsbad is the closest medical position. They need the income because Harry has only a G.S.4 pay ranking, which gives him "the distinction of being the lowest-salaried full-time employee in Guadalupe Mountains National Park." Regardless of his abilities, he can't advance higher, since only managerial jobs pay more and Harry will not sit behind a desk for more than a few minutes at a time. Head Ranger Roger Reisch has also foregone several administrative advances in order to remain in the Guadalupes rather than shuttle up the federal hierarchy toward Washington, but the situation is more dramatic with Harry. Despite his degree in natural sciences, service in Vietnam, five years as a forester and another five as a ranger, Harry is about to be placed under a new supervisor, who is twenty-three years old and was recruited out of college last year as a federal administrative trainee. Now he carries the same G.S.9 ranking as Reisch. The traditional resentment of the veteran line officer for his newly commissioned West Point commander is alive and simmering in the Park Service.

This morning, Michael and I are headed up McKittrick with other photographers drawn here by the fall foliage. We pass a busload of El Paso fifth graders on a field trip snapping away with Instamatics, then a group of geology graduate students from Lubbock, reading the canyon walls below the empty peregrine eyries like a drilling core. El Capitan is

Maple tree against a rain-slicked wall
of Pine Spring Canyon.
Arca Swiss 4 × 5. 210 mm Schneider lens.
Ektachrome.

Maples and saw grass in McKittrick
Canyon.
Arca Swiss 4 × 5. 210 mm Schneider lens.
Ektachrome.

the best preserved dry barrier reef in the world, and its compressed sediments, their layers opened by erosion cuts, have yielded nearly five hundred species of fossils, whose remnants telescope the reef's 25 million-year sequence of marine life. McKittrick is the primary field site for Texas Tech's geology department, but students studying the strata here could just as easily be from anywhere in the world, since comparable formations are found only in the nearby Glass Mountains—the description of whose brachiopods alone fills six thick Smithsonian volumes— and Australia.

Because it is so long, with great changes in moisture and altitude, the canyon is a kind of floral core sample as well. There are no abrupt biotic frontiers here, and each group of plant species flourishes, overlaps, and then like Neapolitan ice-cream flavors, melts evenly into its neighbors, better suited to the next, higher mile of freer water, thinner air, and rockier soil.

In the fall, the desert floor beyond the mouth of the gorge is covered with little yellow Southwest rabbit bushes. Most of the year, their nondescript gray clumps look remarkably like the miniature foam trees used in scale-model railroad layouts, but after the first frosts, especially when the sun is low, *Chrysothamnus pulchellus* lives up to its name, which means beautiful golden shrub. With the yellow foliage come ripened seeds, and white-tailed lark sparrows flit back and forth between the bushes, pecking at the pods. Cold weather also turns the agaritas (*Mahonia trifoliolata* in the prairie and *M. haematocarpa* on higher ground) a hard slate blue that makes them stand out from the gray-green sage and stunted juniper into which they have blended all summer. Their berries are red and swollen just before Christmas, and a few people continue to boil them for jam.

Inside the mouth of the canyon, it is still desert, and the creek is dry, but even the open valley there is more sheltered than the desert beyond, for the Chihuahuan biome is so severe that, although there is no surface water this far below the springs, just being in the lee of the outer canyon walls makes for a marginally cooler environment that enables the plant community to diversify. Even prickly pears and walking-stick cholla do better here, spreading broader purple blooms in early summer and bearing more little radishlike red fruits in fall than more exposed plants just beyond the valley. Scrub oak and red-berry juniper live all the way to the dryer edge of the moisture ecocline, next to the thirstiest of the Mexican orange or zorrillos (*Choisya dumosa*), which are more common farther up the canyon. Small, bent ironwoods are also found in the lee of the bluffs, bearing the pedigree name of Knowlton Hop Hornbeam (*Ostrya knowltonii*). The name derives both from the tree's discoverer, Frank Hall Knowlton (1860–1926), and from the fact that its brown fruits look like malt hops. The reddish-brown heartwood is harder than that of any other local tree and, like similar densely fibered trees all over the world, it is called an ironwood. Its slender, crooked branches won't make lumber, but they are good for fenceposts and whittling into tool handles, furniture legs, and windmill sucker rods. Hornbeam is also good firewood and was favored by blacksmiths for its hot, long-lasting flame, although to burn it today would be a travesty.

Deeper in the canyon, the vegetation is taller, and I realize that I am no longer able to see over it as I can in the open desert outside, where nothing botanical is willing to stick up very far into the fierce, desiccating wind. Alligator junipers (*Juniperus deppeana*) appear, with bark that looks as though it has been uniformly scored with a square-grid waffle iron. The edges of the waffles curl up like dry paper, and when the tree is cut they flake off altogether, leaving a smooth red underbark which, unlike that of any other conifer, bears more resemblance to the skin of an exotic ornamental. Within two miles, by the canyon's fork, junipers are the predominant forest tree. Growing poorly alongside is their boreal antithesis, the white-limbed madrone. Madrone limbs are white because their pale sapwood is exposed through a stringy shawl of outer bark, which the madrone periodically sheds along with its leaves. The sapwood has a velvety texture, which, combined with the tree's round, curving limbs, gives it a steamy combination of common names: Naked Indian and Lady's Leg.

In early summer, oblong panicles of ten to fifteen tiny white flowers cover the madrones, followed four months later by clusters of BB-sized red berries which, in falling, stripe the bark and stain the sand maroon beneath the groves. Everything eats the berries, ripe or not, and every pile of mammal scat along the trails is crumbly with the undigested seeds. The quality of the fruit varies from tree to tree, but those with the fewest berries are usually the sweetest, since birds quickly strip the best-tasting trees, leaving the bitter ones heavily laden for the raccoons and ringtails. Although in large quantities the fruit is purported to be hallucinogenic (the Mediterranean form, *A. unedo*, was the legendary tree of knowledge, and berries from the species' northernmost stand in Ireland were used in Druid ceremonies), the raccoons never seem particularly ethereal, even during the height of berry season in early November when they live on practically nothing else. A number of old recipes detail the making of madrone preserves.

Most of the madrones grow in a marginal habitat on the lower edge of the juniper forest where it is really too dry for them, but because they can't compete successfully with the conifers for the better-watered upper-valley growing sites, they hang on, nonreproductive, in the lower reaches of the canyon. Meanwhile, the moisture continues shrinking away to the north as it has, all over West Texas, for four thousand years. The moisture has remained longest in the high country, and where the madrones can find sheltered enclaves there, free of competing evergreens, they grow largest and most abundantly. Although scattered madrones are present all over the Guadalupe Mountains, they do better in milder climates, and the farthest they can follow the diminishing moisture northward through the high country is a protected canyon twenty miles above the park near the back road to Carlsbad.

Even in the best mountain enclaves, however, madrones are de-

clining. Although trees from higher elevations produce more red berries than the stands in McKittrick, only a few of them germinate, and, of those that do, none passes the seedling stage to replace their elders. Why the species has lost its procreative élan is the subject of everyone's theories. For one thing, madrone seedlings need a symbiotic root fungus to micorrhizae. Like many plants, they can occasionally survive without it, but then they grow slower and are more susceptible to disease and environmental damage. Drought is another culprit, as is heavy grazing pressure by goats and deer, which nibble down the seedlings. Even watered and protected young plants fail, though, despite nets of chicken wire set up by the rangers around the McKittrick Canyon saplings. Experiments on freezing madrone seeds for varying lengths of time are also underway at the U.S. agricultural station in El Paso, on the theory that the trees' reproduction may be geared to the longer winters and wetter summers of the last glacial epochs. At the other extreme, Texas Tech botanist David Northington theorizes that madrone seeds must be exposed to fire before they can germinate strongly enough to propagate the species, and forestry experiments at San Marcos seem to bear this out. For some of the conifers, of course, fire is an absolutely necessary part of the reproductive cycle. Without forest fires, the cones of the jack pine (*Pinus banksiana*) remain tightly shut for years. Only after intense heat has burst the cones apart by turning the moisture within to expanding steam are the seeds released, dropping onto the newly charred ground that is both ideal bedding turf and largely free of competing vegetation. How the madrone seeds might gain from exposure to flame is not known, but fire is abhorred in Guadalupe Mountains National Park and, unless the rangers slip up, the failing resident trees will never get to test their mettle in a conflagration. It may not even be necessary, for healthy seedlings grown on Edwards Plateau ranges not recently burned suggest that fire has little to do with successful germination other than opening a sunlit space, of which there is no shortage in West Texas. Whatever the cause of their decline, though, when these aged trees fall, there will be no more.

Above the junipers, the forest is denser, with fewer species. There is a pattern of differentiation that gives tropical seas fewer individuals, belonging to a larger array of different forms than northern oceans where uniform macroenvironments favor a handful of dominant species, each with millions of individuals. The pattern appears in riparian communities as well. Tropical- and temperate-zone deciduous woodlands offer environments for hundreds of kinds of trees, while the great evergreen forests that ring the northern hemisphere from polar barrens to central plains are comprised of only a handful of types. The Pleistocene remnant forest that fingers down the Rockies into the Guadalupe uplands and fills McKittrick's highest cul-de-sacs is an extension of this old boreal community, and besides aspens (*Populus tremuloides*), now confined to a couple of the shadiest valleys among the peaks, the forest holds only two groups of trees. The oaks include a number of small, predominantly high-altitude forms, the most common of which is the

The red and yellow bark of a Texas madrone glistens after a summer rain.
Arca Swiss 4 × 5. 90 mm Schneider lens. Ektachrome.

chinkapin (*Quercus muhlenbergii*). Gambel (*Q. gambelii*) and scrub oaks (*Q. turbinella*) also grow here, as well as the rarer *Q. undulata, Q. pungens, Q. mohriana, Q. grisea,* and *Q. arizonica.* All of them are closely related, and hybrid oak combinations are fairly common, offering identity enigmas to *Quercus* buffs. The other trees are evergreens: Douglas fir (*Pseudotsuga menziesii glauca*), ponderosa (*Pinus ponderosa*) and limber pines (*P. strobiformis*).

The Douglas fir that still grows in the higher Guadalupe valleys is the Rocky Mountain *glauca* variety rather than the yellow-needled Pacific Douglas fir common on the northwest slopes of the Rockies, comprising 60 percent of the country's second-growth timber. These Rocky Mountain firs have dark blue-green foliage, and their wood is not quite as strong as that of the Pacific trees, although it is better to work since it shrinks and warps less. In the Guadalupes, its quality became an academic question before the turn of the century, since by then all the large, accessible firs had been cut and hauled out to the sawmill at Queen, near the state line in New Mexico. Queen is now a ghost town, surrounded by a gargantuan gray stubble of old stumps, most of them thicker than even the biggest high-country trees.

Limber pines really are limber, with plump, slippery needles and bouncy branches that droop almost vertically with the heavy weight of high-altitude snows. They droop so steeply that the snow slides right off. Even in ice storms, the trees' oozing antifreeze sap permeates its needles and forms a thin layer of slush that keeps them free of the grip, and weight, of ice. It is almost impossible to break off a branch of limber pine, and the trees stand green and unflocked, periodically shaking their dark coats like bears, when the less Arctically adapted ponderosas are buried under thick pillows of drifted snow.

Despite their name, ponderosa pines are often small, even as adults. Along the top of the Guadalupes' eastern scarp, narrow furrows of soil are pocketed between the rocky ridges, and ponderosas compete for a place there so vigorously that they stand only a foot or two apart. Sapping each other's nutrients stunts their growth, and none of the trees attains a trunk diameter of more than four inches. Where the soil is deeper, ponderosas grow ninety feet tall. They are the largest and most common conifers in the southern Rockies and can be distinguished by the raised, puzzle-shaped chunks of their bark, separated by bright orange jigsaw furrows. A single branch may carry both clusters of small cones, which are male, as well as large singles, which are female.

Most of the Guadalupes' pigmy evergreens, however, are piñon pines. They specialize in sparse soil and never grow trunks larger than ten inches, even after two centuries. Their needles are proportionately tiny—only a fifth the size of the largest ponderosas' spiky six-inchers. Piñon cones are round and contain the oily nuts that the Mescalero ground and mixed with mashed acorns and mescal hearts to form agave bread. The nuts are bitter but edible, although they are rough on the teeth. It only takes one pineconeful to make it clear why the first part of an Apache to wear out was his molars.

For there to be a creek in McKittrick Canyon at all is something of a geologic anomaly. Water issuing from springs in most igneous, granite-based desert mountains has little opportunity to flow above ground because the porous sands immediately soak it up. The Guadalupe aquifer, however, drips its spring-borne ground water down limestone bluffs whose calcareous matrix is dissolved and redeposited—as crystalline calcium carbonate—in a hard travertine paving, called *tepetate*, along the streambeds. It looks like lumpy, green-speckled cement. McKittrick Creek flows out of the mountains in a salt-and-green-pepper-tiled *tepetate* aqueduct of its own making. At least, some of it does. In 1943, a flood swept out of the high tributary canyons, carrying Volkswagen-sized boulders—which are still wedged along the banks—that crashed down on its bed like wrecking balls, splitting the paving and allowing half the stream's volume to slip away through the cracks. Another major flood, in September 1978, upended ten-foot slabs of the travertine and spilled 90 percent of the remaining creek into the porous rock below.

Considering all that has been lost, a surprising amount of McKittrick Creek remains, nevertheless, and where its *tepetate* remains intact the stream pools above small waterfalls, with sawgrass surrounding the deep water. Like the rest of the canyon's foliage, sawgrass seems oddly lush and tropical here, for *Cladium jamaicense* is more often found in Florida and the Caribbean, where, like the redtailed hawks, it was first seen and named by European explorers. The pools buzz with dots of aquatic life, but the only ones I recognize are the waterstriders. Sunfish angle out from the banks for a look, but the introduced rainbow trout and fast-water Arkansas largemouths always hide.

On the creek's banks is a deciduous forest dominated by bigtooth maple (*Acer grandidentatum*) and little walnut (*Juglans microcarpa*) right along the streambed, while velvet ash (*Fraxinus velutina*), lowland chinkapin oak (*Quercus muhlenbergii*), and southwestern chokecherry (*Prunus virens*) fill the rest of the valley floor. The chokecherries grow right up against the canyon walls, especially in gloomy overhangs. Their intense, purple fall foliage makes an imperial border around the pale ash and dark red walnut leaves. Above the chokecherries, rock clematis (*Clemantis columbiana*) strings its way up the bluffs. It is a high-altitude plant, able to pop out bluish-white April blossoms at 10,000-foot elevations, so that the sheer rims of McKittrick, 2,800 feet above, present no obstacle. Its more mundane lowland relatives include the roadside Drummond clematis and their city cousin, the oriental garden clematis.

When the first heavy frosts sweep down McKittrick in late October, most of the maples turn orange. Some turn red, and a few are livid maroon. For the next three weeks, the woods look like Vermont, including sightseers, except that the trees are shorter. The canyon is filled with people who drive from all over the Southwest to see the trees, but there are no lines of automobiles idling through the groves because the nearest maples, ashes, and walnuts are a mile beyond the parking lot, and everyone walks in to see them.

Although it looks like New England, almost all the trees are Rocky Mountain species:

> *Similar deciduous woodland occurs from the Grand Canyon and Wasatch Range of Utah across the Mogollon Rim of New Mexico to the Capitan Range of eastern New Mexico, then in a number of canyons south to Sabinal Canyon on the Edwards Plateau, Limpia Canyon in the Davis Mountains, the Chisos Mountains, the Sierra del Carmen Ranges, the Serranias del Burro in Coahuila, to the Chiricahua Mountains in Eastern Arizona, the Animas Mountains in southern New Mexico and the majority of the larger ranges of the Chihuahuan Desert as far south as San Luis Potosí. Pollen records indicate that these forests were much more extensive as recently as 4,000 years ago.**

By mid-November, the maples' gold foliage has become a flamboyant carpet beneath bare branches and a bright mosaic across the pools in McKittrick Creek. The light reflected from the surface is saturated with color, and it is one of Allender's favorite subjects. This morning, however, he hardly gives the floating leaves a glance. Inflamed by the rangers' tales of deeper eddies inhabited by bigger rainbow trout, and the lushest foliage this side of the Cascades, he is drawn by a greater lure: North McKittrick. It is new territory for him. He tried the trail several months before and got sidetracked in a dry wash, assuming that nothing lay in the upper portion of the canyon, but the previous afternoon, poring over a topographic map of the area, he discovered his error and, with it, a whole new section of back country to see. The rangers get a kick out of Michael's enthusiasm, and they embroider their descriptions for him. It's fine with Allender. He wants to believe, and this morning he is having a hard time balancing his vision of Shangri-la in the glen beyond the bluffs with the demands his courtesy requires him to satisfy in plugging along slowly with me. Fretting, he waits at every stream crossing while I catch up. I am both slow and looking for the woodpecker holes which house the canyon's rare miniature pygmy and flammulated owls, but Michael's vague interest in the search is an automatic gesture of courtesy peeled from the center of his focus on the imagined high valley ahead. At the canyon's fork, he finally takes off on his own, attacking the first barrier—a down of fallen trees barring the way north—like a steeplechase pony. I watch through binoculars as he forces over the tangle; a final glimpse of the black nun's cape trailing behind his camera is the last I see of him for five days.

Almost a year later, we are camped on the rim above North McKittrick, veterans by now of the back-country terrain that in the first months here seemed so forbidding. A thousand feet below, the streambed twists a white thread along the bottom of the canyon. It is dry; the

Oaks and maples on a grassy hillside in Dog Canyon.
Nikon FE. 28 mm Nikor lens.
Kodachrome.

---

*P. S. Martin, *The Last 10,000 Years: A Fossil Pollen Record of the American Southwest* (Tucson: University of Arizona Press, 1963).

trout are all over in South McKittrick after all. But the maples, choke-cherries, and walnuts are as thick as the rangers promised. To the east, the land drops away to the Pecos plain through a pair of craggy medieval headlands that split the gorge into a trident of tributary canyons. Caves sprinkle dark blots across their rock faces and, wherever wrinkles offer shelter from the press of wind, narrow stands of maple shoot tendrils of red up the subcanyons. In between, the evergreens are punctuated by fields of bright ocher scrub. The plants are stubby Emory and Gamble oaks, a foot or two high, but from even a short distance their dense mat looks like bracken.

The high-country forest is seldom thick, and here at the northern end of the park the ridges are broader on top and paved with red sandstone smooth enough to move across readily. Not far from camp, the trail along one of the crests shows a line of small mountain lion prints, the size of my palm, at sunup. By ten, the wind has erased them. Just beyond, I cross over the Guadalupes' spine and, starting down the western side of the divide, get a glimpse ahead through columns of juniper and ponderosa to see only clouds. The edge of the escarpment is just beyond the trees. As I break through the last of the stunted evergreens curled away from the steady gale, the wind shoves me back a step, then floats the flat rocks I sail out over the abyss like paper planes, flipping the smaller ones back over my head into the thicket. Below, despite the bright sun, everything is slightly murky. The distances are so great that it is like looking out of an airplane, with all the details of cactus and sage blurred together in a mirage of indistinct dots. One of the details is Allender himself. He is visible mainly because of his huge camera pack and tripod, slowly making his way up the road to Dog Canyon, closed for several months to vehicles. The larger dots of three elk move off before him, grazing intermittently, but not feeling alarmed enough to break for the foothills on either side of the valley. I can't see the turkeys, but farther up the gorge, he tells me that a flock of eleven, not wanting to leave their flightless pullets, trotted ahead of him for nearly a mile between the fences before scrambling off en masse under the wire and down an arroyo.

Three miles westward, across the valley, the sharp ridges of the Guadalupe foothills hide the salt flats, with only the tips of the two tallest of the Cornudas Mountains protruding above the rim, while far to the north, where the dark slopes of the Rockies wrinkle the horizon, Sierra Blanca Peak is visible when its snowfields catch the sun. The lesser Sierra Tinaja Pinta, Black, and Sierra Diablo desert mountains are rough lumps on the plains to the southwest, and beyond their horizon, on nights of high overcast, the reflected lights of El Paso glow dimly, but the gale off the bluffs scours away any feeling of seeing even reflections of the work of man.

Allender grew up in Dalhart, but he won't even visit the Panhandle now because he hates "the dullness of all those miles of nothing but red dirt. . . . the flatness of people's lives." He doesn't go to the lucrative

Amarillo or Plainview art fairs, driving instead to shows as far away as Phoenix or Miami on those weekends. The two places he remembers with pleasure in the Panhandle are the big dirt canyons he hung around in outside Dalhart and the genuine Palo Duro Canyon south of Amarillo. They were the best he could do in the way of topography on the high plains, but they didn't compare to the real mountains he first saw as an eight-year-old, trout fishing with his dad near Red River, New Mexico. Allender was hit with the Rockies' profusion—"I couldn't believe there was so much; so much water, so many trees, all kinds, and such neat high mountains"—and never recovered. Life in the canyons was a stopgap after that, but Michael didn't realize until later that along with the bleak Panhandle vistas, he was also rejecting the psychological homogeneity of the region's pragmatic, utilitarian approach to making a living in oil, cotton, insurance, or sorghum. Allender started becoming an artist twenty years before he first tried to draw.

In the Guadalupe peaks, he again has an island oasis, and the visual patterns and images he extracts here are less scenery than a sense of what is important to him about the wild. It is a romantic perspective, essentially false here, where every foot of terrain is carefully managed land and far from true wilderness. But Allender's feeling for the country is as true to a particular part of its reality as the charts and maps, which delineate its geological contours, catalogue its recreational value, and diagram its future, are to another part of that reality. This is still empty, high desert country, where the extremes of sun and wind and radical temperature fluctuations are what matter most in daily life. They have become largely irrelevant elsewhere, so defeated by technology and our adaptation to the flat commercial urban world that our adolescent wildernesses—dirt canyons seaming the sorghum fields of the Panhandle or creek bank hideouts in the center of a metropolis—are all that most of us ever see of our origins, but they are not enough for Allender.

Along the Manzanita–Pine Spring trail, he is completely immersed in the pale shimmers of gama grass bent by dark waves of wind which turn silver as they cross the pond before us. What keeps him from these scenes most of the time are the shows. Kids are the worst part. "Two or three hundred hours on a drawing and some brat spills a Coke on it," Allender mutters. He does not like children and has a glower designed to drive them away, although it only works with the timid ones so far. The bolder kids, cold drinks in hand, still light on him and his scratch-board display as casually as grackles on a scowly Halloween pumpkin. He waggles his engraving knife at them a lot, but it's usually a futile gesture. The commercialism of his traveling exhibit—"a sideshow in a circus"—is offensive to Allender's sense of quiet decorum. Crowds are hard on sensibilities tuned to mountain solitudes, searching the silence for the click of a hoof, the flicker of a wing. "I absolutely hate to sell myself and my work, but it's competitive; there's only so many dollars that walk in the door, and we're all vying for them. That's why some personalities are so much more successful at this than I am."

McKittrick Creek in upper South
McKittrick Canyon.
Arca Swiss 4 × 5. 210 mm Schneider lens.
Ektachrome.

Foliage and sky reflected near the
headwaters of North McKittrick Creek.
Arca Swiss 4 × 5. 210 mm Schneider lens.
Ektachrome.

Susan accompanies him to some of the shows. "She's shy, too— helps me set up and take down, go get pictures, but she's no salesman, either. That's how come I do demonstrations. I'll just set up a drawing and work on it during a whole three-day show." Michael's precise detailing takes a long time, and always draws the same comments: "'The patience of Job! That must take the patience of Job!'" Michael mimics his matronly patrons. "Well, here's old Job all right, ladies, slugging away." Then the association, the analogy that brought the memory of the art shows to Allender's mind erupts as he breaks into a trot against the confinement of the narrow trail: "Well, that's all I'm patient about; there's too much here to miss, with my head bowed over a table."

Nonsequitur notwithstanding, time is especially precious to Allender. His eight trips a year to the Guadalupes are bought by making millions of tiny dots on large stiff sheets of paper. The primary sales appeal of his drawings is the extreme realism possible only with a technique that Allender developed, combining scratchboard with pen and ink. In order to define every detail of fur, feathers, or bark, Michael lays down a thin layer of black ink in a rough silhouette. Then, using a narrow engraving blade, with infinitely tiny slices and scoops he cuts away most of this matrix, exposing the white china clay beneath. Individual strands of fur, filaments of feather and bark remain. For grass, foliage, sky, and smooth surfaces like water, Allender uses stippling. He creates an entire background—all the incredible visual complexity of a grassy field or leafy forest floor—only with dots. In varying densities, galaxies of tiny, pinpoint dots shade all his tones and highlights. Eight hours yields about three square inches of detail. A finished drawing takes about eight weeks, with stippling eating up two-thirds of that time. Allender's customers are buying realism detailed beyond that of any photograph, but they are also acquiring a laboriously formed artifact, like cottage frame lace, crewel, or embroidery.

The problem is his temperament. The tedium of his skill is provoking to Allender, for while he makes his living as a patient craftsman, what really drives him is an unspoken awareness of how little time there is to catch the light on an insect's spiky legs or glowing through a cactus petal. It is knowledge characteristic of people who have nearly lost the light and are more aware than most that they have only the present in which to function. A tumor several years ago required the emotionally rending experience of major chest surgery, and the aftermath of radiation therapy left Allender's heart sheath heavily scarred. This cuts his wind some, although he still climbs past other hikers on the steep switchbacks, and it serves as a constant, visceral intimation of his own transience. Allender's voracity for the experience of the mountains is that of one who has seen his end, as calm and undaunted as a gutshot hawk. Reprieved, he is still undaunted, but hungry, not with the reckless experience-appetite of a kid, but rather with the edacity of an older gourmand who wants as much of what he loves as possible. Now. (His second passion is cooking, campfire and home, and his specialties are indulgent, better-than-sex chocolate cake and lemon meringue pies not even his mother can equal.)

Allender's other problem is with the limitations of his genre. Like cowboy art, successful wildlife painting requires such idealization of its subjects that the artist's conceptual choices are limited. Only stylized, perfect-specimen game animals and birds, raptors, and cuddly rodents and raccoons in appealing poses interest the majority of the buyers. Within these limits, art is out of the question, and commercial success becomes largely a matter of comparative technical abilities between skilled illustrators, although the intense realism the best of them achieve obscures this romantic cast. As with western art in general, the enormous attention paid to accuracy by both wildlife artist and viewer is a comfortable way of looking past the romantic distortion of formulating natural scenes in human terms: marketing pictures on the basis of the pleasant memories—crisp autumn hunts for the most part—that they call up.

Accuracy is an appealing criterion in this millieu because it is easy to apply, but you can look at a million western paintings and never see a cow paddy. Like the patrons of western art, buyers of animal paintings have so far been unwilling to grapple with the ambiguities of a richer aesthetic. There are no Ansel Adams, Bill Ratcliffs, or Philip Hydes in wildlife painting; the field is too narrowly defined. Michael knows that he is more technician than artist, but he is as much of an artist as his market will permit.

Photography offers a way around the impasse. The fundamental craftsmanship is easier to learn, more widespread, and therefore less valued than the rare ability to render exact detail in wildlife drawings. Lots of people can take technically accurate photographs. What distinguishes the great ones is the intelligence of their conception. It is a tougher field, a bigger league in which to compete, but it is the next logical step for Allender.

The best optical quality is still beyond the capabilities of even the finest 35mm instruments, however. Allender uses an Arca Swiss monorail view camera that records its images on big metal framed transparency plates. The lenses are German—Schneider—a 90mm wide-angle and a 210mm long lens. With a multitude of adjusting knobs and levers flanking the eleven-inch accordion chamber, the mechanism reminds me of the huge box cameras I remember from old photographs, carried on the heads of Martin and Osa Johnson's porters into the African bush at the turn of the century. There is also a bulky tripod and long black focusing hood, or nun's cape. The set-up is more streamlined than Matthew Brady's flashpan arrangement, but it still bristles with the ungainly archaic simplicity of the finest optical instruments. There are no automatic adjustments. Under the hood, the photograph appears upside down on the lens plate, looking exactly the way it will on the final transparency, four inches by five. With its focal plane adjustable horizontally, as well as able to be angled in two planes, the Arca Swiss permits the virtually constant depth of field focusing that is impossible with a 35mm camera. The only penalty for this precision is weight, which on Allender's forays into the high country includes several pounds of 4″ by 5″ metal film frames in addition to the 70-pound camera pack, 20 pounds of food and camping gear, and 25 pounds of water. The camera rides with its spiky controls cushioned against a foam pad lashed to the tripod lying across his shoulders above his blue Kelty pack; and the whole assemblage makes an impressive sight as Michael swings along the mountain trails, loaded like a Sherpa.

Maple leaves collected by a sotol and maidenhair ferns near Smith Spring.
Arca Swiss 4 × 5. 210 mm Schneider lens. Ektachrome.

Maple leaves in a pool near second crossing of McKittrick Creek.
Arca Swiss 4 × 5. 210 mm Schneider lens. Ektachrome.

9

July 10, 1969

Bullsnake. I saw one bullsnake 50 yards NE of log cabin in the bowl. 12:00 P.M. Four feet long. Damn near stepped on him. If my horse Blackjack hadn't nudged me, I would have.

—R. REISCH
GUADALUPE MOUNTAINS NATIONAL PARK
WILDLIFE FILE: REPTILES AND AMPHIBIANS

FROM GUADALUPE PASS, it is nearly eighty miles to the Rio Grande. The river is invisible behind brown shale hills, but beyond it the blue mountains of northern Chihuahua, where Pancho Villa outmaneuvered Blackjack Pershing and the U.S. cavalry in 1916, shimmer through the haze, reminding me of the old Spanish Mexican Southwest that stretches back here more than four hundred years. There is almost always a haze between the border and Guadalupe Pass because of the waves of radiant heat rising from the salt flats. They are the basin of an old Tertiary lake which never had an outlet, so that the residue of minerals washed down from the highlands collected there and dried into salt deserts. The flats are empty now, white and crusty in summer and dotted with milky alkaline ponds in winter. The water tastes bitter and supports only saline-tolerant animals like brine shrimp, but it still draws flocks of waterfowl from the central flyway every fall. Sandhill cranes also stop here on their way to the Gulf Coast, leaving big splayed footprints that, in the rainless desert, still lace the edges of the aquamarine sloughs when the birds pass northward again in March, heading for their Canadian summer homes.

It is no longer worth anyone's while to mine the lakes, and nobody has dug salt here since the twenties, although there are hundreds of acres of it lying around. Until the turn of the century, however, the salt meant life or death to the Mexican farmers who lived over in the Rio Grande Valley beyond the foothills; and they fought, and won, a war for it. Their opponents were the Texas Rangers.

In 1877, El Paso was called Franklin. A few hundred Anglos lived there, just up the river from the larger Chicano settlement at San Elizario. Salt sold for seventeen cents a pound, delivered. Delivery was the only reason to pay anything at all for salt, since it was free for the taking a quarter-mile north of the stage road to Pecos and Fort Stockton. Along

Screech owl (*Otus asio*)

the way was Hart's Mills, where coarse chunks of the lake bed were ground to table consistency. Chicanos dug and hauled the salt, and the Anglos of Franklin bought it, mostly for preserving beef and tanning hides.

Luis Cardis was the first to see the potential in unclaimed flats of seventeen-cents-a-pound salt just after the Civil War, and, although he didn't want to mine them himself, he thought the lakes might be rich enough for him to garnish a fee from the peasants who made their living hauling it from the flats. In hopes of getting them to go along with this, Cardis enlisted the aid of their priest and his business partner, Antonio Borrajo, and together they claimed the salt lakes, ostensibly to protect them for Father Borrajo's parishioners. Before the pair were able to enact any levies, however, they were blocked by State Senator Albert Fountain, who wanted title to the flats vested in El Paso County, which he represented. Fountain's political clout was enough to stalemate Cardis and Borrajo for six years (throughout which the salt miners had no idea of the struggle that was being waged for the right to charge them), until Charles Howard rode into El Paso in 1872.

Howard was a big, tough, back-country Missouri lawyer, who figured the law was what the books said it was and nothing more. To the Chicanos of San Elizario, the law was the people—the custom—and to break the custom with laws and deeds was almost certainly to incite a rebellion. (Thirty-seven years later, this point of view put Villa and Zapata into Chapultepec Palace after the *campesinos* were ordered off their deedless farms by President Huerta.) Mining the lakes was not only the peasants' heritage; it was all that stood between them and starvation. When the Rio Grande ran dry, which it did frequently, their crops died, and the farmers could not live without the buffer of income from their salt deliveries.

Howard's opponents in the salt wars were originally his allies. Cardis had handled Borrajo's financial affairs, which were of considerable magnitude, for several years, and Charlie Howard seemed to be tough and smart enough to take over the legal side of things, especially since he could be counted on to oppose Senator Fountain—a natural enemy of Howard due to the senator's staunch Southern Democrat political persuasion. By calling a few favors due in Austin, Cardis and Father Borrajo were able to pressure Howard's appointment as district judge through the state legislature within two years. Then they made the mistake of letting him in on their plans for the salt lakes. Fountain had left town after being wounded in a saloon brawl a month before, so the way seemed clear for a coup. They didn't plan on a double-cross, however. As soon as Cardis told Howard that the salt lakes were open to claim, the judge filed on them himself. Enraged, Father Borrajo gathered his peasants in the white-arched courtyard of Mission de San Elizario and told them that Howard was about to steal their salt.

In a perfect display of *hubris*, Howard then made things easier for Borrajo by riding into San Elizario, armed with his notarized deed, to

Western escarpment of Guadalupe
Mountains from salt flats.
Nikon FE. 55 mm micro Nikor lens.
Kodachrome.

face down the mob. This got him thrown into a cellar for three days, until he promised, under threat of death, that he would voluntarily "let the courts decide who owned the salt lakes, leave the country within twenty-four hours . . . and confess to 'unjust, improper'" conduct.* Howard knew his promise wasn't enforceable, but his pride was still severely damaged by the assault, and, since he couldn't reach Borrajo, safe in Mission de San Elizario, the judge galloped back into town and, point-blank, blasted Cardis in the chest with both barrels of a twelve-gauge shotgun that he borrowed from the sheriff's office. Then, Howard and his servant, Wesley Owens, drove calmly down the main street in a buggy, out through the badlands of New Mexico to Mesilla, ninety miles west of Franklin.

Astonishingly, no posse set off in pursuit. Nobody, including El Paso County Sheriff Charlie Kerber, was sure of just what had happened in Schutz's dry goods store where Cardis was shot—at least not sure enough to tangle over it with a gunman as good as Judge Howard. Kerber was a county-level career law enforcement officer who wore rumpled black suits and was too wise to go against a gunman much better than himself. He decided to wait for enforcement procedures to go through channels and was delighted to hear, several weeks later, that Governor Richard Hubbard had ordered the Texas Rangers to Franklin. Kerber thought the Rangers, with their flamboyant Stetsons and scarves, were silly adventurers, but he was glad to substitute their bravado for his own.

Getting the Rangers to Franklin proved to be difficult, however. The Butterfield Stage was scheduled to arrive three times a week, but it usually had to fight its way past Apaches and outlaws and was, therefore, undependable. When it did get through, the trip took two weeks. The quickest way to West Texas was to ride the drovers' cattle trails three hundred miles up to the railroad at Topeka, Kansas, pick up the Santa Fe to Ruidosa, and take the reliable stage coming eastward into Franklin from New Mexico. In the end, only Maj. John Jones arrived in the border town in the best "one riot, one Ranger" tradition, and during the month he spent in Franklin, he and Kerber mustered a rough local group of twenty recruits, led by former handyman Johy Tay, which was commissioned as the Frontier Battalion of the Texas Rangers on November 12, 1877.

All this was fine with Judge Howard, who, after his stay in the cellar, was glad to see a little law and order shaping up, and he welcomed Jones to Mesilla. The judge could afford to be affable because he wasn't much worried about his upcoming murder trial, due to the testimony of his friend, Ben Powell, that Cardis had unholstered a pistol just before he was killed—which would have legally made the shooting a duel. And he needed the Rangers on his side to back him against Borrajo's salt miners. With this in mind, Howard even scouted around

*C. L. Sonnichsen, *The El Paso Salt War* (El Paso: Texas Western Press, 1961), p. 28.

Mesilla and found Major Jones another two recruits before riding back to El Paso to post his bond.

Meanwhile, counting on Howard's promise, the miners had returned to their trade. The fall harvest had been sparse, and early in December a wagon train of sixteen big schooners and sixty yoke of oxen left the valley on their monthly haul to the Guadalupe basin, manned by many of the mob that had held the judge hostage two months before. But Charlie Howard was both a hard man to intimidate and a slow learner. When the judge heard what was going on out at his claim, he called up Tay and the Frontier Battalion and, brandishing his title to the salt flats, persuaded them to accompany him all the way to the lakes, if necessary, to enforce his property rights. The group never got past San Elizario.

There, the Ranger company was besieged by angry villagers, waiting for the return of their salt wagons, who drove the company into a barricaded house at the north end of Main Street. It was the Alamo all over again, with hopeless odds. The Rangers even got a messenger out, who galloped into Fort Bliss with news of the siege. It didn't do the captives any good, though, because the fort was only a small outpost and the best it could manage in the way of a rescue mission was a little band of fourteen soldiers, including an unarmed musician, all on foot, commanded by twenty-two-year-old Capt. Thomas Blair. When he got to San Elizario, Blair looked at the hundreds of angry rioters, had a conference with their leader, Chico Barela, and prudently decided that Barela was correct: the battle with the Rangers was local and civilian, not military, so he turned around and marched back to Fort Bliss, leaving Judge Howard and the Ranger company still barricaded in the town.

The group had been under siege for four days when they learned that Captain Blair had abandoned them. They learned it from a pair of militant Franklin mothers who drove into San Elizario and blustered their way past the rebels. Mrs. I. F. Campbell was there to take her daughter-in-law and grandchildren, innocent bystanders, out of the war zone. Mrs. William Marsh was there to get her son Billy, youngest of the Texas Rangers, out of the trouble his leaders had gotten him into. Both ladies succeeded, except that at the edge of town the astonished Chicanos finally decided that Billy was big enough to be a threat after all and threw him into a cell for the duration.

Inside the Ranger quarters, there were now only nineteen men, including Wesley Owens, who, being black, was unarmed; John Atkinson and John McBride, two of Howard's friends; and another innocent bystander, Deputy Sheriff Andy Loomis of Pecos County, who wanted to go home. Tay asked the opposition's permission for him to leave. Since the rebels only wanted Judge Howard anyway, they were glad to see the garrison lose another man, and they threw Loomis into the cell with Billy Marsh as soon as they got him alone. Dividing the Rangers up one at a time like this was working so well that the rebels promised freedom to all the Rangers if Howard would again renounce his claim to the salt. The battle for the salt lakes seemed hopeless by this point, so Howard

The western escarpment below
Guadalupe Peak from upper Bone
Canyon.
Nikon FE. 55 mm micro Nikor lens.
Kodachrome.

El Capitan and the southeastern
escarpment of the Guadalupe
Mountains.
Nikon FE. 28 mm Nikor lens.
Kodachrome.

gave himself up, hoping to save the Rangers, and marched out alone under a white flag. Lieutenant Tay followed, still trying to negotiate, although neither of them could speak Spanish well enough to offer, much less strike, a bargain. Grinning, the rebels sent for John Atkinson to translate: three fewer Anglos barricaded in the compound, three more in the stockade. That afternoon, rifles pointed at his back, they sent Atkinson back to lure the others out. "Everything is peacefully arranged. You will not lose your horses or guns. Tay is waiting. Come on down!"* Incredibly, the Rangers bought the story and surrendered.

The next day, the rebels marched Judge Howard, McBride, and Atkinson in front of firing squads. Then they let the Rangers go, keeping only their weapons. "In the name of Texas, I demand our arms," announced Tay.† The rebels laughed. Except for Barela's intervention, the Rangers would have all been killed in their cells.

Back in El Paso, Tay found a newly assembled band of Texas Rangers: the Silver City Brigade. When Governor Hubbard heard that his Frontier Battalion had surrendered to Mexican rabble, offering up their civilian charges—including a district judge—to execution, more or less in exchange for their own lives, he proclaimed in a press conference that the situation was out of hand, and he wired Rutherford B. Hayes that Texas was being invaded by Mexican nationals. He also wired Sheriff Kerber to assemble a posse. Kerber and Major Jones had already recruited everyone they could find in El Paso County into Tay's Ranger company, but the sheriff knew there was an abundance of martial talent just up the road in Silver City, New Mexico.

A lot of gunsmoke had hung in Silver City's thin air, including some from William Bonney—by then a veteran of the Lincoln County wars—who added a notch there (the sheriff) before going to trial in Mesilla. By 1877, the mines were past their prime, and the town was full of empty saloons and men long on reputation and short on silver. The kind of employment that Kerber was offering didn't come along very often, and the sheriff immediately had himself a flinty-eyed thirty, mostly gunslingers.

Considering what had just happened with Tay's Rangers, Governor Hubbard was dubious about his latest frontier battalion and decided to send in a company of regular army troops just to make sure. But he underestimated the rebels. By the time Col. Edward Hatch, fifty-four infantrymen, and two howitzers got to West Texas on December 19, the enemy had swelled to five times their original number, drawn up on the road to San Elizario. Poorly armed, the Mexican rebels gave way immediately to the combined firepower of Hatch and his howitzers and the sharpshooting Silver City Brigade; but they didn't give up, and when Tay's Texas Rangers, who had regrouped the original Frontier Battalion

---

*Ibid.

†James B. Gillette, *Six Years with the Texas Rangers* (New Haven: Yale University Press, 1963), p. 170.

and joined forces with Hatch, captured several of the rebels they recognized from the siege at San Elizario, and then were bold enough to execute men who had released them only two weeks before, peasants from all over Chihuahua rallied to Barela's cause.

A charismatic figure with glittering blue eyes, Barela inspired the same sort of loyalty that fueled scores of Mexico's grass-roots-bandit revolutions. Although he could have sparked a Mexican-American War, Barela had only joined the fight out of a personal grudge—his daughter had been engaged to Cardis—and his only objective now was salt. Because Hatch's artillery was too potent to face head on, the Chicano leader knew his only option was to wage a long war of attrition, and, adopting the universal tactic of rural revolutionary armies, he dispersed his peasants into the Mexican countryside and began guerrilla raids across the Rio Grande.

The raids took less of a toll than the stress of holding together an army of gunfighters. Unable to pursue their furtive adversaries across the border, the Silver City Rangers stewed in frustration, finally announcing that they didn't need to pay for anything at all in San Elizario, especially wine. The telegraph wire reported that federal investigators were on their way, via Topeka, but nobody paid much attention. A couple of the gunslinger rangers raped the sister-in-law of Juan de Dios Aldrete, one of Howard's enemies. Then they began to plug each other. On New Year's Day, First Sergeant Ford shot First Sergeant Frazer; and as other bouts shaped up, the war receded into the background.

With this, the governor backed down. The title holders to the salt were all either dead or departed anyway, and he had to muster the Silver City Rangers out of the Frontier Battalion in a hurry, so Hubbard took a diplomatic approach, proclaiming, "Both sides to the controversy are more or less to blame; what has been done cannot be undone, and the restoration of order is now the prime requisite."[*] What was left of the Silver City Brigade broke up and headed for Denver, Kansas City, or back up to the mining towns of New Mexico, as Tay's Rangers returned to their jobs in El Paso. From Chihuahua, the peasants filtered back into San Elizario once more, and were soon making monthly salt hauls to Franklin; while Father Borrajo, still undiscovered as one of the original conspirators, was moved by the Bishop of Durango to the smaller parish at Guadalupe, where he adopted a very low profile.

---

*Ibid., p. 171.

The southern wall of McKittrick
Canyon with the Permian Basin
beyond.
Arca Swiss 4 × 5. 210 mm Schneider lens.
Ektachrome.

A skylighted, rain-slicked wall in
Dog Canyon.
Nikon FE. 55 mm micro Nikor lens.
Kodachrome.

Michael Illender
©'80

10

May 31, 1967

*Merriam's Turkey: 1 hen and six eggs. One mile from bowl. South
McKittrick. The hen left her nest when a horse party went by. She never
came back. Eggs did not hatch. Nest of pine needles and twigs on the
ground.*

       —R. REISCH
       GUADALUPE MOUNTAINS NATIONAL PARK
       WILDLIFE FILE: BIRDS

O N SATURDAY MORNING, Pine Spring campground is a hub
of activity. Groups of backpackers, already signed out, wait in line at the
trailhead leading to Guadalupe Peak (left fork) or Pine Top and the bowl.
Each party gives its predecessor about fifty yards' headstart before setting out. While the hikers wait, they chat with Roger Reisch. Reisch is
the chief ranger at Guadalupe Mountains National Park, and he stands
by the trailhead on weekend mornings to encourage the hikers as they
depart. He is also watching for potential search-and-rescues. A group of
Boy Scouts from St. Luke's Methodist Church in Midland arrives in a
white school bus. The parking lot is level, but, as soon as the bus stops,
scouts assigned to wheel duty leap out and chock all four wheels with
big rocks. Each of them carries a hiking stick cut from a broom handle.
One kid has his gear in a plastic garbage bag, stretched to transparency
and hanging down over his rear.

 "How many in your bunch?" Roger askes the troop leader. Then he
counts them. "You'll make Guadalupe Peak okay, maybe four and a half
hours if you take it easy. Watch for snakes!" The garbage bag will break,
but Roger won't have to haul the scouts out. Before the next group
advances to the jump-off point, Reisch is on his walkie-talkie. He raises
Harry Lord, stationed halfway up the peak. It is about their twentieth
conversation of the morning. Harry notes the scout party's departure
time, estimates when they will pass his position, and confirms that the
first hikers to leave the camp that morning have just gone by him in
good shape. Then he tells Roger not to worry, which he knows is point-
less. No one has seen Mike Allender, who has been in the back country
for days now.

 Between hikers, Reisch fumes about fires and communists. "One
guy builds an outlaw fire (any campfire not in a stone Park Service

Turkey (*Meleagris gallopavo*)

fireplace], and they all want to. Just like communists. They say, 'We saw those other folks had a fire,' and you know what I tell them? 'The jails are full of murderers, too—you want to go kill a guy because somebody else did?'" Reisch is middle-aged, muscular, florid. He wears a flat-brimmed ranger hat from which, in hot weather, a red bandana is draped like a legionnaire's neck flap. It is not hot weather now and, without the kerchief, Reisch's uniform looks exactly as though it is covering Smokey the Bear. He becomes more agitated as the next party of back-packers arrives: three scruffy, bearded, Austin types in tennis shoes, carrying their water in plastic orange juice jugs. By the time they reach us at the jump-off point, Reisch is Mark Trail again. They turn out to be in good condition, experienced hikers, and they ask Roger where to go. He is as cordial to them as to the pair of young executives who have just passed, trailwise and expensively equipped. "Up Pine Canyon to the bowl: real beautiful country, evergreens and oaks, then you can drop back down through Bear Canyon. It's steep, seven and a half miles in all, but you guys will be coming right over that saddle there"—he sights it out for them—"about dinner time. You'll be hungry, too. I've got a girl ranger stationed up in the bowl if you need any help." Before they have gone a hundred feet, Reisch has notified Caroline that they are on their way. They were better prepared than he had anticipated, and Roger seems relieved—no potential search-and-rescues so far.

No dogs either this morning, but Reisch noses around the motor-homes just to be sure. "People sometimes leave Dobermans—killer dogs—in their campers. A medical doctor did that at Easter. I was here the whole two days he was gone in case it got out." Dogs are not al-lowed in the back country, and Roger tries to catch them at the trail-head. Only one has ever gotten through—an Irish wolfhound—and Roger grins, remembering how the owner put one over on them. "He got by us, outlaw camping in the woods off the trails all the way across the park." Reisch's respect for the guy's wilderness skills is stronger than his lawman's instincts. "And no fires, I will give him that. I don't think he made any fires."

Reisch has never married. He has no family here and seldom so-cializes with his ranger staff. He is completely wrapped up in Guadalupe Mountains National Park, and its future as a wilderness area is his overriding concern, in part because his past here stretches back into the last years of cattle, sheep, and goat ranching in the high country, years before the park was established. Except for heavy grazing, the land fared well as Hunter Ranch property. Almost no one got to see it, of course, except ranchhands and Reisch, who rode its trails as a stockman with hard-bitten, old cowhands like Hunter's foreman, Noel Kincaid; but the mountains remained wild. Now they are owned, and fairly heavily oc-cupied, by the public; and different forces control their destiny.

For those like Reisch, to whom preserving what remains of the Guadalupe wilderness is important, the issue divides along conven-tional liberal-conservative ideological lines: does wild country survive better in public or private hands? (Photographer Abe Blank moved to

Texas because so much of its land is individually owned. He hated the human impact—detritus as well as occupation—he had found in the public lands of Colorado and California. Here, he blithely slides through barbed wire fences onto private ranchland and enjoys the use of millions of unoccupied acres. He carries cameras and a butterfly net, on the theory that "no one shoots a guy catching butterflies." Often, this ploy is not even necessary, for Abe is well educated, well spoken, and has impressive credentials—he carries along a couple of *Ranger Rick* magazines featuring his material—and even without trespassing he can usually gain entry to at least some of the ranches in any area he chooses. Michael is at the other extreme. He is too shy to ask strangers to let him use their land and would rather drive a thousand miles than cross another man's fence. That leaves only public land, and the scarcity of it in Texas is pushing him west, to live in Utah or Washington.) In the short run, private ownership of remote ranchland is almost always less harmful than the substantial park traffic of rangers and backpackers, especially since the future of the big parks includes engineered access by means of scenic tramways, paved overlooks, and, outside their federal boundaries, the spreading ring of commercial Dairy Queen sprawl that has grown up on the peripheries of national monuments from Mammoth Cave to Yosemite.

In contrast, so much of Texas has remained wild so far because it is private, mostly the property of big-spread stockmen who are in a better position to protect the land from overoccupation than the administrators of any public park. One of the reasons they can do this so well is their long-standing allegiance with the Texas Department of Parks and Wildlife, which is run by a six-member commission that has historically consisted almost exclusively of wealthy ranchers whose first interests lie in protecting the game, privacy, and eminent domain of their fellow large-scale landholders. Their protection comes primarily from the department's 325-member law-enforcement body of game wardens, each equipped with a .357 magnum revolver. Parks are also the department's domain, but the board has always been slow to acquire land for public use, and wildlife on private property has always received the bulk of the commissioners' attention.

Much as this rankles an egalitarian consciousness, keeping the public at bay like this might be the best way to keep the back country wild, even if nobody but a few wealthy owners and their hands got to see it. If the ranchers were truly independently wealthy, it might be; but even the fattest wallets are ultimately under the control of the marketplace, and no land in Texas is *terra incognita* on the developers' charts. It's just a matter of time until the price is high enough, for ranchettes and residential resorts are just too profitable; the alternative agricultural life, too hard. It is happening all over the country, of course, scenic areas first. The huge, wild ranches of Montana's Big Sky and the central Colorado valleys were relatively safe under the old cattlemen that ran them before the First World War, but their sons and sons-in-law today are real estate men. They are concerned with environmental quality, greenbelts,

Early fall colors of bigtooth maple
against saw grass in North McKittrick Canyon.
Arca Swiss 4 × 5. 210 mm Schneider lens.
Ektachrome.

Smith Spring on the south face of the
Guadalupe Mountains.
Arca Swiss 4 × 5. 90 mm Schneider lens.
Ektachrome.

and preserving limited tracts of "wilderness." Their children will build condominiums on the hillsides.

In Texas, during the last five years, much of the hill country and even West Texas has been bought by large corporations based in Houston and Dallas. The land's highest value is still as rural recreation, because turkey, deer, and dove hunting is now the lagniappe of corporate business. The land still looks the same—juniper brakes and open range—but its future has changed. In a few years, economics will dictate other uses for these corporate assets, and they will be converted into agricultural, commercial, or rural residential properties as smoothly and with as little regret as bonds draw money from the stock and real estate markets when interest rates slide upward. To the men who will make these conversions, the idea that the creatures who live on the land have a prior right to it is ridiculous.

Public land is less susceptible to pressures from the real estate market, if only because the federal bureaucracy seldom lets go of what it controls; and the "this acreage is just too valuable to hang on to as rangeland any longer" argument has more tenacious opponents in this arena than the tenuous resolve of an indulgent or bankrupt private property heir. The problem is in looking after it.

"You simply cannot buy public land and then leave it in the bank, let it sit idle without development. The public will destroy it. They'll use it for a garbage dump, cut the timber on it. It's a shame, but we have to protect that land from the public," Pearce Johnson, former chairman (twice) and current premier member of the Parks and Wildlife Board, argued in a recent interview. (Johnson's own ranch is well looked after, incidentally: one of the magnum-toting wardens lives on it.)* He is right on target about the cost, though. Managing public land takes a lot of people, and money, even at idealistic park ranger pay scales, and state or federal equity-oriented government officials are reluctant to approve funds for its protection without receiving in return some sort of facility that provides public access to the land. And access is the thing that separates big-time parks from backwater ones, well-paid career civil service staffs from crews of underequipped, part-time helpers. Even the most windswept ranger wants to be part of a first-class operation, although few seem to be aware of the implications of this sort of pride.

A couple of the more ecologically oriented Guadalupe Park rangers, and Reisch, see the importance of totally isolated wilderness as the earth's primary genetic bank, but it's definitely a minority viewpoint. Although park terrain may never be commercially zoned, it is also unlikely to receive the protection it deserves as remnant wilderness. Few rangers are naturalists. They are advisors, helpers, monitors, rescuers, and occasionally policemen to the backpacking public, and they deal almost exclusively with people. To them, and to virtually all of even their most hard-core hiker constituents, wilderness is a place for

*Richard Starnes, "The Texas Fat Cat Game," *Outdoor Life*, February 1980, pp. 132–133.

151

people to go; an opportunity for a challenging workout in partially simulated mountain-man conditions. The rangers don't want their protectorate overtrammeled by hikers, but the land is open to the public and more people show up every month. The staff is obliged to show them the park, and, despite minor grumbles about vandalism and the hassle of rescue missions, for the most part they are delighted to do it. Visitors are the park's valued customers, and competition for media exposure, advertising, and public attendance is keen between parks, especially here where highly developed Carlsbad Caverns forty miles up the road draws high attendance figures—and correspondingly large federal budget allocations—while Guadalupe Mountains must scrounge harder for its draw from the demographically smaller hiking public. The walls of both parks' administrative offices bear large charts marking their respective visitor scores, month by month, and everyone roots for the curves to keep mounting. Mostly, it is jobs and salaries that are at stake, but the same competition for status and the benefits of bigger/ better that fuels corporate rivalries also operates here. To the satisfaction of nearly everyone, park attendance has finally reached a level high enough to warrant the construction of a new visitor center, whose existence, it is hoped, will boost the turnout even higher. To the conservationist, this is not what the wilderness is for.

"We would like to keep the Forest Service out of the wilderness, and, for that matter, the National Park Service, too. They build too many things for their own convenience . . . ," maintains former Sierra Club president, Dave Brower. "If ten percent of the land is still wild, we should tithe with it. Man has taken enough for himself already. We should pretend the rest doesn't exist. It's there for a different purpose."*

But it is not the purpose of most of our society. Ultimately, of course, whether public or private, all protective stewardship of the wilderness is futile   building campfires in front of the human glacier in Robert Vines' analogy. Energy shortages notwithstanding, under the inexorable pressure of our constantly growing numbers, people are steadily pressing outward from the cities, and much of today's open country is already locked within the ice of next year's blueprints. More acres of the United States are now paved than are held in parks, national and state. Reisch knows there is no such thing as a permanent victory— a battle won is only a delay, a campfire lit before the ice—but a loss means the disputed wilderness is dead. No one tears up asphalt; once civilization has taken hold, it periodically rebuilds its structures, but it never retreats.

Although the glacier will not recede, eventually it must melt, if only because no species is immortal. Meanwhile, like Brower, or even Reisch, some continue their existential battles as holding operations, well aware of their long-term futility.

---

*John McPhee, *Encounters with the Archdruid* (New York: Farrar, Straus & Giroux, 1971), p. 71.

Fallen ponderosa pine needles among
leaf litter in a pool in Dog Canyon.
Arca Swiss 4 × 5. 210 mm Schneider lens.
Ektachrome.

Dead maple tree after a light
snowfall in McKittrick Canyon.
Arca Swiss 4 × 5. 210 mm Schneider lens.
Ektachrome.

Guadalupe Mountains National Park's trail network—eighty miles—carried 26,000 hikers during 1978. Guadalupe Peak and Pine Canyon alone were walked by 7,633 backpackers. None of the paths are designed for hiking. They are cowtrails left over from the Hunter Ranch that were cut into the mountains to let cowmen on horseback reach their stock in the high country. Because of this, they are steep, rocky, and prone to erosion. Reisch worries about both the trails and the hikers. His job is often similar to that of an air traffic controller, working with very erratic pilots. Its stress is evident to all the rangers:

"Roger chronically overreacts."

"He has an impossible job, but no one else could do it as well."

"Roger really cares about the park—it's just that it can't be protected like he wants."

Saturday afternoon, what Roger has been dreading occurs. A pair of hikers report trouble up on Guadalupe Peak. Far above them, they saw two packers far off the trail on a narrow ridge. One man thinks they yelled, "Hello," but his companion believes it was, "Help!" The pair drive away, while Carole Bryant fiddles with the central radio, calling Harry, who is now on his way down the mountain. She didn't get a map location from the men, and Harry needs a fix on the lost hikers. "I'll try to intercept the guys who saw them at Pine Spring. They're in a green Renault. I know because I filled out their permit." About halfway through this exchange, Roger blasts in—he monitors all walkie-talkie exchanges—ordering Harry to round up a couple of good climbers, three hundred feet of rope, lanterns, and climbing gear. A minute later, he's back on the horn: "Where the hell is Allender? Anybody seen him? Isn't he supposed to be down by now? Didn't have enough water for this long did he?"

"No." "No." "No."

Because Reisch takes his responsibilities as seriously as if he were maneuvering jumbo jets through a traffic pattern, hikers often feel the consequent tension of being shuttled along pathways from monitor to monitor. It is strangely regimented to set out into a rugged western canyon knowing you will be checked by a spotter within a half mile of your car.

"Why not operate like a Baskin Robbins, Roger? Set a quota of a few thousand a year and, when your number comes up, you go—few enough people to leave everyone a little freer?"

The answer is official. "The Park Service has not set a maximum-use number for our area. We are open to the public."

Then it is unofficial. "Whenever you limit the public's access— their use of some resource—in the park, you have to get it through the Congress. Ten or fifteen people a day are plenty to be going in to Smith Spring [4,621 registered at its trailhead in 1978], but, hell, I don't have that authority. When we get the funds for good trails, though, and I mean twenty-seven–degree grades, thirty inches wide, smooth surfaced, with water bars—you'll see a lot less erosion."

Even on top, this is desert country and vegetation recovery rates are slow. Of course, erosion can only be halted; there is no recovery.

"But those good trails are bound to bring in a lot more hikers. Wouldn't you rather leave them rough and limit access that way?"

Roger laughs at my naïvete. But it is a small laugh because he wants the park kept wild too. He gives me a copy of the Park Service Act and shrugs. The future of the park is simply not up to him.

Reisch's boss is Area Manager Bruce Fladmark, and, beyond him in the chain of command, a long string of administrators leading up to the country's top ranger, Russell Dickenson, head of the National Park Service. The eighty thousand acres of Guadalupe Mountains National Park may be Roger's Ranch to local residents, but it's a speck in the 35 million acres under Dickenson's supervision, which accounts for 1 percent of the land area of the United States. It is managed by fourteen thousand people: administrators, supervisors, rangers, naturalists, historians, and, in Washington, D.C., policemen and janitors. Dickenson is, in turn, responsible to Interior Secretary Cecil Andrus. In this bureaucracy, Reisch is atomistic, invisible. At Guadalupe Mountains National Park, policy comes from Washington, and only Reisch's intense presence can cushion the public impact on the region's wildlife. It is a tenuous, temporary defense.

The best that even Reisch can hope for the park's future may be something like Rocky Mountains National Park—broad thoroughfares leading through a shaped, cultivated, and meticulously cared-for wildernesslike setting, but a different world from the raw peaks and dark forests of the Never Summer range, one ridge of Rockies to the west Here, parts of the adjacent Lincoln National Forest, just over the state line in New Mexico's Sierra Blancas, are also a different kind of place, and wilderness compared to much of the park.

But it is vulnerable wilderness. Although the Sierra Blancas are still empty enough for elk and bears, it is only because the enormous size of the national forest has dissipated most of the human impact so far. Compared to Guadalupe Mountains National Park, there is virtually no protection of the land, however, and the part that is accessible is not holding up well. Jeep trails cut the woods, with blackened campfire rings marking the clearings every half mile along them. In summer, clusters of orange and blue tents spring up like Day-Glo mushrooms, and, in fall, hunters jounce over the ruts, wider every year with their passage. Two of them, in a rifle-racked Chevy Suburban, rumbled across our camp one morning, leaving four-wheel-drive tracks between the stove and sleeping bags. We had found mountain lion prints three hundred yards away the day before.

Similar usage problems confront the park. No roads cut into its back country yet, but everyone wants to influence how the mountains will be used. Unlike private acreage, the public has a say here, and there are a thousand conflicting says, each with a different interpretation of what the park should be. Its administrators are the focus of intense

Autumn colors two miles from the
mouth of McKittrick Creek.
Mamiya Super Press 23. 2¼ × 3¼.
100 mm Mamiya lens. Ektachrome.

A natural arch in McKittrick
Canyon.
Mamiya Super Press 23. 2¼ × 3¼.
100 mm Mamiya lens. Ektachrome.

opposing forces—from preservationists like Brower to commercial developers with plans for adjacent motel-restaurant "support complexes," hard-line traditional ranchers to vague mountain commune builders—most of them lobbying diligently for their own version of the Guadalupe wilderness. In the middle is Roger Reisch. The land he manages for the public, using rules sent out from Washington, was long owned and only bitterly surrendered by the Culberson County ranchers who have been Roger's lifetime neighbors and friends. It is tough to cut against their antigovernment grain. What the local ranch folk claim to resent most about the Park Service is that it "cares about fish and animals but not people." They fume about rivers in Arkansas "left undeveloped because of a silly little fish" and tell each other how the government can't take care of all the wilderness it already has in Alaska. What really bothers them, however, is that the park destroyed the old hierarchy of which they were the aristocrats. The new land barons are federal employees, and their camper constituents are outsiders, city people new to the area and initially not well received. A local service station refused, for awhile, to sell gas to people who looked like outsiders.

Reisch is one of the few old hands in the Park Service, and in style and temperament he is more rancher than bureaucrat, although his awareness of the fragility of the wildlife here is far beyond the stockmen's primarily economic perspective.

"Our first priority, of course, is the protection of human life," Roger tells me, right out of the handbook. "But our springs are the most vulnerable spots in the park." Protection of their life is a lot more interesting. "There are jillions of little creatures, crustaceans and what not, up in those pools, that have been there since Pleistocene times. If people walk around the edges to get a drink—like they want to after climbing all the way up there—they mash down the moist area those creatures need to lay their eggs. It changes the water's turbidity and, therefore, the temperature, heat transfer, and its rate of flow. Without those crustacean and insect eggs, some of the bird species would have no prey . . ." He pauses to emphasize this point, knowing my interest in raptors, "And the peregrines who feed on those birds would be gone.

"Moths pollinate the yuccas. God, I don't know what all the connections are, but it's just a giant web; everything's connected, and if you start pulling one part the whole thing unravels." Reisch fiddles with the mike to the master radio, quiet for a moment. Silence is unusual for him. "The hardest thing is to tell people to just settle down and look . . . see how everything fits together. I hate centipedes—big old things eight inches long—I used to kill every one I saw. Now I just sweep them out of the way."

As we talk, a dull boom rattles the little frame house at Frijole every few minutes, puffing out a tiny cloud of chalk dust high on the ridge to the west. A thin line of raw limestone slices across its face to the site of the blasting: the new trail up Guadalupe Peak, thirty inches wide, graded to National Park Service specifications.

Both the National Park Service and its boss, the Department of the Interior, call the Park Service's substantial real estate holdings facilities and chart the public land within them according to various zones of use, the most protected of which are the primeval areas. Guadalupe Mountains National Park is a primeval area, but Section I, Paragraph 4, of the National Park Service Act declares that "wilderness features within any primeval park shall be kept unmodified except insofar as the public shall be given reasonable access to outstanding spectacles." In the Park Service, reasonable access is the one underlying principle honored more in the observance than the breach because, along with restrooms, it is the feature most in demand by the facilities' visitors. In Yosemite, before the shuttle trams, access meant a million cars a summer idling along in each other's exhausts, making one big U-turn through the narrow valley. Here, money permitting, reasonable access would mean a three-thousand-foot cable car ferry to the top of Guadalupe Peak.

"As of now, I think the cable car issue is pretty dead," Area Manager Bruce Fladmark concludes tactfully. "Not that it would be a bad thing. If the funding should come through, it would show many more people why we have a national park here, including the young, the aged, and the infirm." Fladmark is the best PR man here. Being more or less infirm myself—the only way my plated and pinned football knees will ever carry me to the top of Guadalupe Peak is through the door of a cable car—I can see his point. I would like to have that view over the desert too. But it would cost the mountain too much. Cable ferries in Switzerland have hauled thousands of tourists, including me, to the top of the Pennine Glacier, doing less harm to the peaks than the scuffle erosion of fewer people scrambling up the steep alpine climbing trails. But we saw only a postcard view from our balcony at the upper terminal. Behind its guardrails, the gale off the snowfields only had a momentary chance at us and no real meaning. I liked even the very small alps that I struggled up alone much better.

Dead issue or not, Roger is still wrestling with the gondola plan. The idea pains him as much as it does Michael.

"Then you know what you'd have? There would be people running out to the edge of El Capitan, throwing their cold drink cans off," he mutters. "There are birds of prey that live on those cliffs. They need the security of height and the solitude to nest. With this deal, you know what they'd get? A rain of aluminum." I know exactly what they'd get. In Arizona, rangers practice mountaineering techniques by rappelling down hundreds of feet from the Grand Canyon overlooks to fill their bags with Pepsi cans, while the slopes below roadside overlooks along the western scarp in Lincoln National Forest are strewn with the same aluminum debris.

So far, though, only peregrines drop from the Guadalupe Park cliffs. Showing off for their mates, the tiercels' derring-do takes the form of giddy display dives which send them whistling down into the canyons, cracking miniature sonic booms as they pull out just above the trail.

While they are at the eyries above Pratt Lodge   usually from the end of April until June—the area is closed to visitors:

May 27, 1978—Peregrine Falcons

Alan Cox and Mark Struble [had] a Celestron s. 1250mm—F10 eft 50-inch telescope and camera [at] Turtle Rock for observing and photos. There were three young in nest . . . mostly covered with white down. Black rings around eyes, wings were dark, almost black. Eyrie is located about 300 feet above floor of McKittrick Canyon.

Arrive Turtle Rock at 8 A.M. and begin observing. Adult birds brought prey in at 8:15, 11:00, and 12:15. The prey was always a bird, but could not identify. Each time adult brought prey it would stay about 5 minutes.

At 2:15 a turkey vulture ventured near the nest and a parent repeatedly attacked it until it flew off.

Each time someone spoke or made a noise from Turtle Rock or above, the parent bird would immediately look at the source of the noise.

If all was quiet when an adult bird brought prey into the nest, they would never look back out. . . . At one feeding a group of backpackers were coming off of Turtle Rock trail. They were not making an unusual amount of noise, but the adult bird was exceptionally disturbed. Every 2 to 3 seconds it would turn its head and look in the direction of the backpackers. At this particular feeding the parent did not stay in the nest over 2 minutes, which was much less than usual.

—GUADALUPE MOUNTAINS NATIONAL PARK
WILDLIFE FILE: BIRDS

Living alone up in the canyon below the peregrine cliffs has given Harry and Sharla a paternalistic interest in the falcons' tentative breeding efforts.

"I don't believe they succeeded in nesting this spring," Harry told me worriedly, "although they had young in '78." Disturbed by hikers climbing Turtle Rock across the gorge from their eyries, the peregrines were badly off schedule: "I hadn't seen the nest yet, but I had hopes for them all spring," he said, "until I saw the male putting on courtship display in May—rather than back in March—long after he should have known it wasn't going to work out. They had a couple of researchers, of sorts, up here from the Chihuahuan Desert Research Institute, and one of them thought it was the female's fault. He said she was a new bird, an inexperienced young hen instead of our old breeder, but he only got a quick look. From seven hundred yards, with them zipping around like swallows, I'd say that's a pretty astute call. After all, at that distance it takes a while to tell one *cow* from another."

During the forties and fifties, peregrines fed on New York City's pigeons, and a few even nested in the dark cornices fringing the top of some old Victorian buildings, but they lived hundreds of feet above the

Maple leaves add their color to McKittrick Creek.
Nikon FE. 55 mm micro Nikor lens. Kodachrome.

sidewalks in the security of height. The presence of humans on their level seems to be one thing that nesting raptors will not tolerate. (The breeding colony of peregrines at Cornell is monitored through peepholes so that the falcons never see their keepers.) Their whole lives—territorial combat, courtship displays, and everyday hunting—involve diving from above on opponents or prey, and they will not accept anything less than an ivory tower relationship with other creatures.

On the paneling above the little stuffed eagle's case hangs the poorly mounted head of another vanished animal here, the desert bighorn. The last ram to live in these mountains, it was shot by Bertha Glover's husband, Walter, near the top of Guadalupe Peak on Christmas Day 1909. Hunter Ranch goats no longer graze in the park, and the montane habitat has improved so much in the last eight years that an analogous species, Aoudad sheep introduced from North Africa by hunting-lease operators, are moving into the bighorn's old niche. They look a lot like bighorns, with full curl bosses on the old rams, except that, among Aoudads, both sexes have exotic Berber goatees dangling beneath their chins. Roger doesn't like exotics in the park and listens, scowling, as Caroline excitedly reports having walked right up to a sleeping Aoudad ram on the slopes below Coyote Peak, getting photographs of him as he bounded away. Reisch doesn't want to see the pictures. He wants to see a carcass.

"Did you shoot him?" he growls. (The Park Service wants to reintroduce desert bighorns here, and an established population of Aoudads, competing for the same limited browse, would make that impossible.) His gruffness is the product of having been on the spot all day. Brushing past Caroline, he squeezes back into the familiar narrow slot in front of his master control radio post, responsibility for the protection of human life occupying every bit of his attention: Reisch has a search-and-rescue forming up among rangers whose battered walkie-talkies receive about half of what he broadcasts to them, as well as growing fears about Allender's long absence and limited water, as he spins the dials of the big continuous wave transmitter, juggling a half-dozen topics as he flips back and forth with rapid-fire intensity between rangers scattered all over the mountains.

The door to Reisch's office does not close—there is a bookcase pinning it open against the wall—and while he works his crackly communications network, the flow of visitors past the reception desk goes on about five feet away. A brisk couple with Ray-Bans comes in, leaving their Dodge Power Wagon idling outside. She is short and in sandals and he is wearing a Caterpillar tractor cap. Both are lean and brown. They want to know about the park's four-wheel-drive trails. Carole says there are none. "But there are beautiful hikes nearby, if you want. Some only take half an hour." She is really trying. They are surprised, disappointed, but friendly. Hiking holds no interest for them and they rumble away, contour maps spread across the dash, rollbar-mounted lights gleaming beneath the thunderheads that, building up behind the peaks all day, are now heavy with nascent hail generated in the turbulent spin cycles set off by the lightning strobes periodically backlighting the clouds' dark faces. Pushed by damp westerlies, they slide off the escarpment, dragging their heavy bottoms across the spiky line of junipers along the rimrock and accelerating the afternoon into dusk. Harry is already wearing a headlamp as he bangs up the steps, laden with foul weather gear for the search-and-rescue. Joe Vinson, stalwart of the ranger team, is mountaineer training in Utah, so Jim Grace and Tony Armijo are called up from a barbecue at Signal Peak. They tumble out of their jeep, hauling rope and pitons. The little Say's phoebe that flits discreetly off her nest on the porch a hundred times a day as visitors pass is frantic with the turmoil. The young rangers are exuberant at the prospect of a rescue mission and almost manage to hide it beneath grumbles about their missed dinner. Harry is methodical. He has heard too many false alarms before and was up on the mountain this morning and saw no trouble: "Roger's unduly upset, but that's a bad storm and Allender's in it right now." Stronger gusts, backed by rain, sweep off the bluffs, rocking the porch as the party sets out. Over the radio comes news that tornado winds have ripped through Pecos, overturning house trailers.

As he readies another team of rangers through the transmitter's static, Roger tells me about their last rescue: a doodle-bugger. These free-lance geological explorers frequently need rescuing because they are drawn to the caves and strange declivities that pocket the Guadalupe scarps. This one found himself trapped on a narrow shelf, his body bowed like a banana around the convex face of the adjoining cliff. "He hung there from ten in the morning until we pulled him off just before dark. Athletic kid, twenty-two years old—anybody else would have fallen. The wind kept shoving him back and forth along the ledge. Wore the soles completely off his boots."

A few weeks before that, the rescue mission was more serious. Early northers had brought a week of twenty-seven–degree temperatures and crisped the maples with color, but the weekend before Halloween was balmy and the park was full of visitors. Five of them were amateur climbers from Texas Tech. Coming down Guadalupe Peak, the last man fell behind and, trying a shortcut across a narrow ridge leading down from the peak, leaned too heavily on a little clinging juniper, which pulled out and sent him flying over a precipice. Fortunately, it was a small precipice, and he landed on a rocky shelf, part way down the mountain, where he lay, conscious but unable to move.

By the time Harry and his crew reached the slag hill below, Roger had cajoled out of the Fort Bliss brass a rescue helicopter, which circled the peak looking for the kid in the darkness. The rangers shined their big lights up at it every time it went over, but so did every camper in the back country, and after whirring back and forth in a confusion of waving flashlight beams for half an hour the pilot headed back to El Paso. It was midnight before a team of mountaineer-spelunkers—able to climb in the dark—arrived from Carlsbad with their heavy alpine rescue gear and drilled a bolt into the cliff from which to swing a pulley and stretcher.

Although thoroughly banged up, with a twisted knee and multiple bruises, the climber was less badly hurt than anyone—including himself—had thought, and he revived enough to help the rangers lower him off the hill. Harry got him out to the roadhead at Pine Spring before dawn.

The radio squawks with news: "Allender is down!"

"How is he? Did he make it to the overlook? Run into any of those bears? Were the pictures spectacular?"

Harry is used to the questions. "I don't know, Roger, he's pretty beat. Been hallucinating."

Twenty minutes later, at the trailhead, I find Michael soaked and exhausted, with minor hail damage, but okay. He is chewing groggily on honey and Granola. His visions immediately strike a sympathetic chord in me: they revolve around a piña colada and a hot tub. Heroic efforts and his own fantasies notwithstanding, Allender is a long way from being a real mountain man. But he had made it to McKittrick Overlook and back on a half-ration of water—all that he could carry beneath the Arca Swiss, its tripod, and the mountain of heavy metal film packs this one-time effort required.

To get there, he had to cross what Roger calls the bear sanctuary. Bears are protected everywhere in the park, but in the dense stands of ponderosa just above the eastern rim, the absence of trails offers them sanctuary from the procession of hikers that pass through McKittrick Canyon below or, to the west, wind their way up Guadalupe Peak. The thicket even smells like bears. Unlike cougars, black bears can live well in a restricted territory if it is rich in food and offers winter shelter, and the thickets and caves along this broken ridge are so well populated with them that, especially in damp weather, their musky scent hangs almost congealed under the dense evergreens.

Crashing through the ponderosas in a futile attempt to reach the peregrine cliffs at the head of McKittrick before his water ran out, Michael was too noisy to surprise any bears, but he slept in a rock field filled with their big humanlike scat piles and dislodged boulders they had overturned in pursuit of gophers and chipmunks. (At the same spot two weekends before, Bill Hicks, a camper from Odessa, looked out of his tent at sunup, right into the face of a mountain lion seated a few yards away.) The second night on top, it took several heavy impacts on his sleeping bag before Michael roused himself enough to peer up into the pines, where a great horned owl perched, contemplating another dive on the faintly moving, billowy nylon worm that had invaded its hunting ground. Exhaustion dimmed his interest, and, waiting for the next attack, Michael fell asleep.

In the morning, with dry canteens rattling at his belt, Allender knew he had only half a day to make the cliffs above upper McKittrick and still be able to reach the springs at the base of Bear Canyon by nightfall. The limits are the same for everyone: how far can you go on the water you can carry? A gallon weighs eight pounds, but the dry desert air sucks away perspiration so fast that it will not last a day. In winter, it is just as dry, but the cold and altitude combine to sap one's strength even faster. So far, the harsh terrain and climate have protected the mountains from man less than their absolute lack of water—the heavy weight of which makes it impossible to penetrate very far into the back country, even with large canteens. (The Katz' archaeological team needed several fifty-gallon barrels of drinking water lifted to them by helicopter in order to remain at their dig in the high country for two weeks.) In the end, more than the resolution of conflicting wilderness ideologies, master plans, or federal Park Service policy, the simple lack of water may keep at least the interior Guadalupe Mountains wild as long as they are dry.

In his van, Allender's snores have begun to reverberate over the slackening rain, and the heavy wind is just breaking up when I see Harry coming off the mountain. He had thought it was a false alarm all along, but the two hikers really had gotten stranded. John Reeves and his companion left the trail about noon on what appeared to be a short-cut—the same traverse across a connecting ridge to Guadalupe Peak that had trapped the climber from Tech five months before. They couldn't see that a narrow canyon cut the ridge off from the big mountain until they had slid down a rock face too steep to get back up. They were stranded but not in danger, and, after spending most of the day there, yelling down at hikers a thousand feet below, they managed to inch their way around the bluff and make it back to the trail just before the rangers got to them. Harry will walk the familiar trail up McKittrick Canyon in a cold drizzle tonight and sleep at home instead of in a wet bivouac on the bluffs. Roger can relax. The first hikers won't leave Pine Spring until sunup.

Shot late in the day with only an f-stop to spare, the photographs were Michael's best so far; his log records the final sequence:

> The clouds were moving in, but the routine was familiar: Release the legs of the tripod, lock them into position. Set it up so one leg points toward the scene. Level the platform with the side legs. Impossible—choose a better spot. Repeat. Choose a lens—the 240 mm seems right for here. Take off the lens shade, remove the 90 mm and stow it, put on the 240 mm. Rack the front standard out and the rear standard back. Open the diaphragm, lock open the shutter. Throw the focusing cloth over my head and take a look. Good balance, but needs to be a little to the left to avoid the branch. Unlock the front slide and move standard to the right. Lock it. Better. Now focus on the horizon and tilt the rear standard back to focus on the foreground. Refocus. Looks good, so lock everything. Take a reading with the meter: on the horizon, on the light cliffs, on the dark cliffs, on the foreground. Good; there's only 3½ stops difference. The wind is occasionally

dying down, so I think I can risk ⅛ sec. Set shutter, then f/
stop for f/22. Close diaphragm, cock shutter, put lens shade
on and rack it out. Open the spring back, take a film holder
out of my belt pack and slide it in. Close pack and check
everything. All looks well. Remove the dark slide, wait for a
quiet moment, let that cloud pass, wait for another quiet
. . . there. Click.

Golden eagle (*Aquila chrysaetos*)